Gentle Ben

Kirsty F. McKay

Published by The Book Dragon Ltd, 2024.

Table of Contents

Gentle Ben 1
Prologue 2
My Rescue 7
Meeting the Family 12
The Curious Case of the Bearded Roommate 18
The Great Bone Blunder 24
A Day at the Seaside 27
The Case of the Vanishing Feline 33
The Day the Law Came Knocking 36
The Tyrannical Landlord 40
Ghostly Encounters 44
A New Home, A New Adventure 50
A Fiery Tail 54
The Mouse House Escapade 57
A Startling Discovery 60
A Picnic Mishap 63
A New Home for the Holidays 66
Ember, the Black Cat 69
A Farewell to a Scaly Friend 72
The Iced Bun Heist 75
Suki's Final Purr 79
Binx 83
The Serenading Puss 87
The Black Dog 90
The Walk 96
Walk on the Wild Side 99
Field of Dreams (and Feathers) 102
Dental Despair 105
Nana Lynda and the Endless Belly Rubs 109

A Tail of Two Terriers 114
The Curious Case of the Coprophagic Canine 120
The Puddle Plunderer 124
A Raisin for Concern...131
Ben's Big Adventure 134
Walking the Walk 137
Diary of a Humper: Operation Sniff 'n Scatter...............143
A Tale of Unlikely Heroics 149
An Unexpected Encounter...155
A Feline Fracas 160
A Final Farewell to a Feisty Friend..................................164
Princely Pampering at the Poochie Palace 167
A Tale of Jealousy and a Monkey's Demise 173
A Picture-Perfect Moment (Almost) 177
Lip Smackin' Good 182
The Wanderer's Return...188
A New Pack in Pandemic Times 192
A Terrifying Twist in Our COVID Tale 198
A Feline Frenzy 203
A Bittersweet Transition 208
The Puppy Invasion 213
Slowing Down 220
The Mailman's Magic Touch 223
The Void Where Companionship Used to Be................227
My Girl's All Grown Up...234
Empty Nest, Full Heart...236
The Return of the Black Dog...239
The Day I Became a Canine Fashion Icon 243
A Gentle Ramble 246
A Difficult Road Ahead 249
Leaning on My Pack..253

The Long Goodbye 256
Life's Greatest Comforts 261
A Heart's Farewell 265
Epilogue..271

Dedicated to our Gorgeous Gentle Ben.

The Happiest Hello and the Hardest Goodbye.

Your Paw Prints are Forever in our Hearts.

Benjamin McKay

11 July 2009 to 17 January 2023

© Kirsty F. McKay 2024 First Edition
Published by: The Book Dragon
6 West Row
Stockton on Tees
TS18 1BT
United Kingdom
ISBN: 9781068628863

This is a work of fiction. Names, characters, businesses, places, events, and incidents are either the products of the author's imagination or used in a fictitious manner. Any resemblance to actual persons, living or dead, or actual events and places is purely coincidental.

All rights reserved. No part of this publication may be reproduced, stored in a retrieval system, or transmitted, in any form or by any means, electronic, mechanical, photocopying, recording, and/or otherwise without the prior written permission of the author. This book may not be lent, resold, hired out or disposed of by way of trade in any form, binding or cover other than that which it is published without the prior written consent of the author.

Kirsty F. McKay asserts the moral right to be identified as the author of this work.

British Library cataloguing in Publication Data. A CIP record for this book can be obtained from the British Library.

Prologue

I meet the teary-eyed gaze of my mistress with my large chocolate brown eyes and try to convey as much love and understanding as I can muster. My look is both her comfort and undoing as the dam breaks. Droplets of salty water land gently on my nose. We both know that the end is inevitable, and whilst I have come to accept this, she continues to struggle with the decision I must trust her to make. My soul would willingly soldier on for the sake of my family if my body had only been capable, but sadly, despite the help of my vet, it is a battle lost.

I can feel the disease tear its destructive path along my spine as it disintegrates piece by piece. The dog I was, I know no more. Although this illness causes me no physical pain, it is no life for me, and I silently weep alongside my mistress.

My legs shudder and collapse beneath me, no matter how much strength I will into them. My paws knuckle and I can sense that something is wrong, yet I cannot physically feel the pain of it. The disease has robbed me of sensation in my rump.

My dignity lies in tatters as I cannot rise or move to let my mistress and master know that I must go out to toilet. I lie in the embarrassment of my own urine leaking from my bladder and faeces from my bowel which is riddled with an illness my vet cannot cure.

I wag my tail as hard as I can, although it too betrays me, and barely thumps on the floor. My apology for dirtying my home as they clean me up and bathe me gently. My master cleans my skin and fur with such care so as not to cause me any discomfort. My mistress whispers words of reassurance that touch my heart. I am grateful that they both understand that this is not me.

The tears continue to roll down my mistress's face as she places her forehead against my own and tells me how much she loves me. How sorry she is that she cannot find a way to extend my time with my family. When she pulls back to look into my eyes, I lick her chin, kissing her softly to say, it's okay. I know she has tried, as I have laid by her feet many nights and listened to her and the master talking. She scrolls through pages and pages on her phone, visiting the different pet websites and forums searching for answers. I know they continue to elude her as she drags her hands down her face and bites down on her trembling lip. Degenerative Myelopathy, the name given to the foreign invader attacking me from within. My ears lift as she reads the findings to the master.

"It is a non-painful progressive disease that causes paralysis in older dogs, a degenerative spinal disease. Starting with one hind limb and subtle weakness, then spreads to the other."

Now there is a name for my 'drunken sailor' walk and the sense that all is not well as my paws drag and my hind limbs cross on the rare occasions I find the strength to walk, causing me to fall to the ground in a matter of seconds.

"The disease progresses quickly, causing further weakness, muscle atrophy, and finally faecal and urinary incontinence."

As it moves along my spinal cord it will eventually affect the forelimbs, and I will be completely paralysed. The prognosis is poor, and the result, my death.

They take me to my vet, seeking hope. A way to slow the progression down, to give me more time. The vet's eyes are full of sadness. No such hope can be offered to my family.

"It is palliative care now. When the time is right, you will know in your heart," she tells my mistress.

The golf ball lodged in my master's throat can be heard as he swallows and almost chokes on his grief. My mistress grips his hand for comfort and furiously blinks back her own grief. But then I see the resolve in her face, and I know that she has made her mind up to make my time left as comfortable as possible. On the way back from the vet we take a short detour, stopping off at the pet store.

My master stays in the car with me as my mistress hurries inside. The minutes pass by and then the door opens. My mistress has purchased yet another dog bed for me, a cushion, and something else that brings a slight smile to her lips.

The master and I are intrigued, but we wait until we are home for her to explain. I watch my family prepare my new bed.

"It is much sturdier," she explains. "It means that we can carry him in and out of the car easier, and allows me to take him into work with me. We are a dog-friendly establishment after all."

"And what are those?" my master asks.

The mistress opens the packet, and he takes them from her hand with a smile. "Are they the right size?"

"I gave the measurements, breed and the weight to the shop assistant and she gave me these," she replies.

I turn my head as the master kneels at my rump and starts to slide the fabric around it. My tail pokes out of a hole in the strange black fabric. They both look at each other and I can see they are desperate not to laugh. I roll my eyes and a snort breaks free from the master.

"He looks like he is wearing a mankini." He explodes with laughter.

The mistress strokes my head and apologises. "I am so sorry Ben, these are supposed to be incontinent pants to fit you but she's given me the wrong size. Take them off him," she tells the master.

But the master is pulling them off already. "Sorry Ben, we will have to find you another pair of Super Pants."

Although it has been at my expense, I did not mind the joke. It was good to see them both laughing, even for the briefest time. No dog wants to see their family unhappy.

The mistress winces in discomfort as she rises from her position and reaches for a cushion on the settee. She places it on the floor and sits on top of it. I pull myself forward with my front paws and lay my head in her lap, knowing what it has cost her to sit beside me. She strokes my head, calls me by my favourite 'pet' name—'Benny Boo'—and tells me it will be okay. For me, yes, my misery will end as I cross the Rainbow Bridge knowing how much I am loved. But for her, the master, and my family, who have all come to be with me, I understand the pain of their grief will continue until the day comes when they can say my name with a smile, feel my love that forever remains with them, despite the sadness of our separation that I know still touches their hearts.

In the vet's small room, I am sedated and sleepy, but I can hear my family's voices and I am not afraid. I feel my mistress holding onto my paws tightly, each member of my family's kiss to the top of my head as they whisper their love and goodbyes. The vet asks my mistress and my master if they are ready. I hear their emotional reply, echoed with my own, and then blackness.

My Rescue

I hear the unfamiliar voices approaching and my ears perk up. Two new people have come to visit. I've already seen a large number walk through the door, then turn and walk away. Some leave of their accord, others are refused by my current owner. 'Chancers,' I hear her say. Apparently they only want to use me for breeding, and she suspects some may have more sinister motivations. Whilst my current home is not the happiest home, at least I know that she does have my best interests at heart.

It is a man and a woman who enter the living room, accompanied by my current owner. The woman immediately breaks into a warm smile upon seeing me as I spring up to my feet. I immediately sense their kindness and hope has me jumping up and down. I am determined to make them want me.

"Oh, look at you! Aren't you handsome!" the woman coos.

"And very energetic," the man says, looking slightly nervous. I can sense his reticence. Even at three years old, I am quite a big dog. But once he gets to know me, he will see how lovable I am.

"How old is he?" the woman asks, giving me a scratch behind my ears.

It is impossible for me to contain my excitement and I wag my tail furiously. I plant my paws on her chest and crane my neck to lick her face. She laughs and gently guides me back down. "What a sweetheart you are!"

Her husband is looking more uncertain as I spin around in circles and leap and prance my way around the kitchen. Finally, I lie down and expose my tummy and wait for a good scratch. I see a smile tug at his face as he kneels, and I know he is starting to thaw. The woman is glancing around the rather unkempt kitchen. I can sense she is taking it all in. The small size, my empty bowls and a dirty lead that hangs from a peg on the wall. My current owner launches into her rehearsed story about no longer being able to care for such an energetic dog due to her work schedule. She explains that I used to belong to her father, who raised me as a pup. But then he died and she took me in. Some of what she tells them is partly true. However, I know that she doesn't lack the time due to her job. She lacks the commitment and desire to care for me, and it is apparent that she has had no training at all on what a dog such as myself needs. I am too much like hard work, and work that she can no longer delegate to her child. He is fifteen human years and is out with his pack most days and nights too.

My owner answers the woman's questions, and I can see in her eyes that she is not best pleased with the responses she hears. I begin to worry that they won't want me.

So I sit obediently in front of her and gaze up at her with my big brown eyes, and I offer my paw. Charmed, she takes it, and I lick her hand. She laughs at me when I do the same for the opposite paw.

"He really seems to have taken to you," her husband observes. But there is a note of hesitation underscoring his words.

My current owner must sense this too. "He is not usually this energetic. We've not long come back from Manchester and he has been on his own."

"How long were you away for?" the man asks.

"Three weeks," my owner replied.

"You left Ben alone for three weeks?" the woman says incredulously. "What about his food and walks?"

"Oh, my neighbour came in and fed him. He let him go outside in the back garden."

I know I must show them, and so I bark and run into the living room.

"Perhaps he needs a wee now?" I hear the woman say, taking my cue.

I knew I was right about her.

The couple follow my owner to the door that leads into the garden at the back of the house. My owner lets me outside and I pee on the plastic covering the lawn.

"Why is there plastic over the grass?" the man asks.

"Oh it's because Ben's pee is ruining the grass, my husband has planted some grass seed down so we've had to protect the lawn whilst it grows."

"I see," the woman replies and I catch the look exchanged with her husband.

"Ben is such a good boy," my owner prattles on. "We've never had any accidents in the house. He just needs a family who can give him the time and attention he deserves."

"Are his vaccinations up to date? Flea and worm treatment? Has he been neutered?" the woman fires a series of questions at my owner. I am really beginning to love her.

As expected, a firm no, to all comes the reply. My owner informs them I only had my vaccinations when I was a puppy. She explains that I am kennel club registered.

"How much do you want for him again?"

"Fifty quid," replies my owner.

The man takes out his wallet and pays my owner the money. Fifty pounds doesn't seem a lot of human money to me. Is that my entire worth?

My current owner pockets the money and then proceeds to find a carrier bag, filling it with my meagre possessions. She clips on my lead and hands me over to my new owners. I am beyond ecstatic and I cannot wait to get out of the door of this miserable life. The woman pulls back on the leash and tells me to heel, but I am not familiar with the command and I continue to drag her to the front door.

My heart leaps for joy when the fresh air greets me.

"He's going to be hard work. Are you sure about this?" the man asks.

"Could you bear to walk away and leave him there? Three weeks alone, what the hell were they thinking?" she replies and throws the carrier bag into the car. "And that crap can go in the bin. I am buying him new."

I can hear she is angry but I know it is not at me. I jump excitedly into the back seat as they attach a smaller lead to my collar and it plugs into a socket in the seat. Restrained, I lay down, my tail wagging and my tongue lolling out.

"Look at him, he's not even expressing any concern about leaving that family. Not a whimper. It's almost as though he couldn't wait to get out of there."

She's right. I couldn't.

The man sighs heavily. "I can't argue with you on that, it was no life for a dog. If you are sure you can manage him, I will support you."

"Thank you," she tells him. "We'll find a way to manage, and with some training he will settle into the family just fine."

I didn't look back once as they drove me away from my former keepers and towards what I hoped would be my forever home.

Meeting the Family

The car finally came to a stop, and I couldn't contain my excitement any longer. As soon as the door opened, I leaped out, my tail wagging furiously. I was ready to explore my new home and meet my new family.

I bounded into the house, my nose twitching as I took in all the new scents. That's when I saw them - three young humans, staring at me with a mixture of surprise and amusement. I couldn't help myself; I jumped up, my whole body wiggling with joy.

"Alright, Alright!" the tall one said, laughing as he pushed me back down on all four paws. I gave them all my best doggy grin and tried again to leap up and lick their faces, but they were not having any of it. That was when I noticed another human, an older lady, standing in the corner. She looked at me with an anxious frown.

"Oh my, he's quite large, isn't he?" she said, her voice a bit shaky.

I heard my mistress call her by her name, Nana Lynda, and I realised she must be the mother-in-law. I wanted to show her that I was a good boy, so I trotted over to her, my tail still wagging. As I got closer, she shrunk back a little. We both hesitated, and then tentatively she leaned forward and gave my head a good scratch. I spun in circles, pleased I had won her over with my doggy charm.

Suddenly, a delicious scent wafted into my nose, and I forgot all about Nana Lynda. My mistress had put down a bowl of food for me, and I couldn't resist. I gobbled it up in seconds, my brain not even registering that my stomach was full. Labradors like me tend to have that problem, but who cares when the food is so yummy?

As I finished my meal, I noticed a soft, green rug on the kitchen floor and I went to investigate it. It felt so nice and squishy under my paws that I couldn't help myself - I lifted my leg and peed right on it. Oops!

"Ben, no!" my mistress scolded, but I could tell she was trying not to laugh. "Do you think he thinks it's grass?" she queried turning to my new master.

"I hope not!" he replied.

The two young male adults, Jacob and Adam, left the kitchen, so I decided to follow them and investigate my new home. I followed Jacob to his bedroom and watched as he made himself comfortable and picked up an object. He turned his attention to the picture box. He looked like he was having fun and so I wanted to join him. I hopped up, my big body sprawling across his lap.

"Mum!" he yelled and rose from the bed. I tried to show him my affection by mounting him, but he quickly pushed me off. "Ben's trying to hump me," he explained with a red face.

My mistress grabbed me by the collar and led me back into the kitchen. She must have sensed that I needed to burn off some energy because she grabbed my lead and took me outside for a walk. I was so excited to explore the neighbourhood, but she kept me on the lead as we walked up the street and into the nearby woodland. I couldn't wait to run free and chase some squirrels, but I guessed that adventure would have to wait for another day.

As we walked through the woods, I couldn't help but be amazed by all the new sights, sounds, and smells. The trees towered above me, their leaves rustling in the gentle breeze. I could hear the chirping of birds and the scurrying of small animals in the underbrush. My nose was working overtime, trying to take in all the fascinating scents of the forest.

I tugged on the lead, wanting to investigate every nook and cranny, but my mistress kept a firm grip. "Heel," she commanded, each time I pulled. However, she did seem to understand my curiosity, and let me sniff around a bit.

As we made our way back home, I couldn't shake the feeling that this was just the beginning of a grand adventure. Sure, there would be some challenges along the way, like winning over Nana Lynda and the young humans. My mistress also explained that she would need to teach me the house rules, but I was up for it all. I just wanted to be liked and loved by them all.

When we got back inside, I flopped down on the cool floor, my tongue lolling out of my mouth. My mistress sat down next to me and scratched behind my ears, and I leaned into her touch, my tail thumping happily against the ground.

"You're a good boy, Ben," she said softly. "I know it's a lot to take in, but we'll all get through this together."

I looked up at her with adoring eyes, knowing that I had found my forever home. And with my new family by my side, I knew that anything was possible...

Just as I was basking in the love and attention from my mistress, she mentioned something about introducing me to the resident cats.

Cats?

I had never met a cat before, but I was always eager to make new friends.

With my tail wagging excitedly, I followed my mistress into the living room. That was when I saw them - two sleek, furry creatures perched atop the sofa, eyeing me with a mixture of disdain and curiosity.

"Ben, meet May and Suki," my mistress said, gesturing to the cats.

I bounded over to them, my tongue lolling out in a friendly grin. "Hi there, new friends!" I barked enthusiastically. "I'm Ben, and I can't wait to play with you!"

May, the larger of the two cats, looked down at me with a raised eyebrow. "Play? With a dog? I don't think so," she meowed haughtily.

Suki, her sister, nodded in agreement. "We don't associate with your kind," she added, her tail swishing back and forth.

Undeterred by their cold reception, I decided to take matters into my own paws. I started jumping up and down, trying to reach them. "Come on, guys!" I whined. "I promise I'm a lot of fun!"

They moved away and I could have sworn I saw them smirking at me, enjoying watching me make a fool of myself.

Determined to win them over, I decided to try a different approach. I rolled over onto my back, exposing my belly in a sign of submission. "See?" I panted. "I'm harmless! Just a big, friendly pup who wants to be your pal!"

May and Suki exchanged a glance, and for a moment, I thought I had won them over. But then, quick as a flash, they both leaped down from the sofa and landed right next to me.

Before I could even react, they started swatting at me with their paws, their claws thankfully retracted. "Take that, you overgrown fleabag!" May hissed, bopping me on the nose.

"Yeah, learn your place, dog!" Suki chimed in, batting at my ears.

I yelped in surprise and scrambled to my feet, my tail tucked between my legs. "Okay, okay, I get it!" I whimpered. "No need to get violent!"

As I backed away from the feisty felines, I couldn't help but feel a little disappointed. All I wanted was to be their friend, but it seemed like they wanted nothing to do with me.

My mistress, who had been watching the whole exchange with an amused expression, finally intervened. "Alright, you two, that's enough," she said, scooping up the cats and giving them a gentle scold. "Be nice to Ben. He's part of the family now."

May and Suki just meowed innocently, as if they had done nothing wrong. I, on the other hand, was starting to wonder if I would ever win them over.

But I wasn't about to give up. I was Ben, the determined Labrador, and I had never met a challenge I couldn't conquer. Even if it meant enduring a few more swats to the nose, I was going to make those cats my friends, one way or another.

As I settled down in my bed that night, I couldn't help but dream of the day when May, Suki, and I would be the best of pals, chasing each other around the house and napping together in the sunbeams. It might take some time and a lot of patience, but I knew that with my unwavering spirit and goofy charm, I would eventually win them over. After all, who could resist the lovable Ben?

The Curious Case of the Bearded Roommate

As if my life wasn't already full of surprises, the following day my mistress decided to introduce another two members of our household. I was just getting used to the idea of the resident cats, when I heard her mention something about 'bearded dragons.'

I cocked my head to the side, trying to imagine what kind of creature could possibly have both a beard and the scales of a dragon. My curiosity was piqued, and I couldn't wait to meet these new additions.

The mistress walked into the living room and uncovered two large glass tanks, that were brightly lit. She beckoned me over. "Ben, come and meet George and Ludwig, our bearded dragon friends!"

I cautiously approached the tanks, my nose twitching as I caught a whiff of an unfamiliar scent. Peering inside, I saw two of the most peculiar-looking creatures I had ever laid eyes on.

George, the smaller of the two, was nestled on a bed of sand, his eyes half-closed and his body looking rather frail. The mistress gently scooped him up and draped him across her shoulders like a scaly scarf. "Poor George. He's a rescue, like you," she explained, stroking his spiny head. "We're going to give him a better life."

I watched in amazement as George clung to the mistress, his claws gripping her shirt. It was a sight to behold, and I couldn't help but let out a soft whine of approval.

Next, my attention turned to Ludwig, who was perched atop a rock, his head held high and his gaze fixed on me. Unlike George, Ludwig seemed to be in prime condition, his scales gleaming under the light.

To my surprise, Ludwig showed no fear of my size. In fact, he seemed to be weighing me up, his eyes narrowing as he assessed the potential threat. "Well, well, well," he said in a raspy voice. "What do we have here? A giant drooling beast, I presume?"

I let out a friendly bark, my tail wagging. "Hi there, Ludwig! I'm Ben, and I'm so excited to meet you!"

Ludwig remained unimpressed, his beard puffing out in a display of dominance. "Charmed, I'm sure," he drawled. "Just keep your distance, dog. I don't do slobber."

Just then, May and Suki sauntered into the room, their tails held high. They took one look at Ludwig and froze, their eyes full of disdain.

Ludwig, it seemed, was not a fan of the feline kind. He immediately started head bobbing, his beard turning a dark shade of black. "Well, if it isn't the meddlesome cats," he hissed. "I've got my eye on you two."

"Time for you to come out too," my mistress said, clearly not noticing the two cats entering the room.

To my utter shock, Ludwig suddenly darted towards May and Suki and chased them around the room. The cats, usually so poised and aloof, were reduced to a pair of frenzied fur balls, leaping, and yowling as they tried to escape the determined dragon.

I couldn't help but let out a bark of laughter at the sight. It was like watching a miniature dinosaur chase down two oversized mice. Even George seemed amused, his eyes twinkling from his perch on the mistress's shoulders.

The chaos continued until Ludwig suddenly veered off course and scampered up the cats' scratching post. He perched himself at the top, looking down at May and Suki with a triumphant glint in his eye.

"Ha!" he crowed. "Not so tough now, are you, kitties?"

As the excitement died down, I couldn't help but marvel at the strange turn my life had taken. Here I was, a Labrador living with two mischievous cats and two bearded dragons - one a sickly rescue and the other a feisty little warrior.

The mistress, clearly amused by the whole spectacle, scooped up Ludwig and placed him back in his tank. "You can come out later when the cats have gone for their afternoon naps," she chuckled.

As the days went by, I found myself increasingly fascinated by our new scaly roommates. George, despite his frail appearance, had a gentle soul and seemed to enjoy nothing more than basking in the warmth of the mistress's affection. He would often ride around on her shoulder as she went about her daily tasks, his eyes half-closed in contentment. He made quite the conversation starter.

Whenever visitors came to the house, they would be greeted by the sight of a bearded dragon clinging to her like a living accessory. Some would yelp in surprise, while others would coo and marvel at the unusual sight.

"Oh my goodness!" one visitor exclaimed, her hand flying to her chest. "Is that a . . . a dragon on your shoulder?"

The mistress laughed, stroking George's head. "This is George, our resident bearded dragon. He's a bit under the weather, so I'm his personal chauffeur for now."

George, for his part, seemed to revel in the attention. He would puff out his beard and tilt his head, as if to say, "Yes, I'm quite the handsome devil, aren't I?"

Ludwig, on the other hand, was a different story entirely. When he wasn't busy tormenting May and Suki, he could often be found perched atop the cats' scratching post, surveying his domain with a regal air.

I would watch in amusement as Ludwig would strut back and forth, his beard puffed out and his tail held high. "Look at me," he seemed to say. "I'm the king of this castle, and don't you forget it!"

May and Suki, of course, were less than thrilled with Ludwig's antics. They would glare at him from a distance, their tails twitching in irritation. But they knew better than to challenge him directly - Ludwig may have been small, but he was a force to be reckoned with.

Interestingly, as Ludwig continued to torment the cats, they began to see me in a different light. Since I never chased them or tried to assert dominance like Ludwig did, they started to appreciate my calm and friendly demeanour. It also helped that Ludwig seemed completely unbothered by my presence, which further convinced the cats that I was not a threat. Gradually, May and Suki became more tolerant of me. They would even brush past me without so much as a hiss or a swat, which was a huge improvement from our early days together.

While they still didn't seek out my company for playtime, they no longer went out of their way to avoid me either.

One day, I decided to try and make friends with Ludwig. I approached the scratching post, my tail wagging tentatively. "Hey there, Ludwig!" I barked. "What do you say we bury the hatchet and be pals?"

Ludwig eyed me suspiciously, his beard twitching. "Pals? With a slobbering canine? I think not."

But I was not one to be easily discouraged. I flopped down on my belly, my head resting on my paws. "Aw, come on, Ludwig. I promise I'm not so bad. I just want to be your friend."

To my surprise, Ludwig's expression softened ever so slightly. "Well, I suppose you're not as bad as those insufferable felines," he conceded. "But don't think this means I like you, dog."

I let out a happy bark, my tail thumping against the floor. "I'll take it!"

From that day on, Ludwig and I had a tentative truce. He would still chase May and Suki around the house, and he would still strut around like he owned the place. But occasionally, he would deign to acknowledge my presence with a nod of his scaly head.

As for George, he continued to be the mistress's constant companion. I would often see her hand-feeding him special treats and making sure his tank was always clean and comfortable. It was clear that she had a special bond with the little dragon, and I couldn't help but feel a twinge of jealousy.

One evening, as I lay curled up in my bed, I heard the mistress talking softly to George. "You're a fighter, Georgie," she murmured. "We'll get you healthy and strong again, I promise."

George let out a contented little sigh, and I felt my heart swell with affection for both. Even though I may not have been the mistress's only companion, I knew that I still held a special place in her heart.

And so, life in our household settled into a new normal. Two cats who had learned to tolerate me, two bearded dragons with very different personalities, and one lovable Labrador - it was an odd mix, but somehow, it worked.

I knew that no matter what challenges lay ahead, we would face them together. Because that's what family does - even if that family includes a grumpy dragon with a penchant for mischief, a sickly dragon who doubles as a fashion statement, and two cats who may never be my best friends, but who had at least learned to accept me as a part of their world.

As I drifted off to sleep, surrounded by the soft snores of my companions, I couldn't help but feel a sense of belonging wash over me. This was my home, my pack, and I wouldn't have had it any other way.

The Great Bone Blunder

Life with my new family was never dull, especially when it came to mealtime. You see, I have a bit of a problem when it comes to food - my tummy seems to have a direct line to my brain, constantly telling me that I'm starving, even when I've just eaten. It's a Labrador thing, or so I've been told.

This little quirk of mine has gotten me into trouble on more than one occasion. There was the time I decided to go trash diving in the kitchen bin, convinced that there were hidden treasures to be found amidst the teabags and eggshells.

"Ben!" my mistress had scolded, pulling me away from the bin by my collar. "That's not for you, you silly dog!"

But I just gave her my best puppy-dog eyes, my tail wagging innocently behind me. It's not my fault that humans throw away perfectly good food, right?

Then there were the incidents with the young adults' rooms. Adam, Jacob, and Bronwyn were always leaving tasty titbits lying around—half-eaten sandwiches, bags of crisps, even the occasional slice of pizza. It was like a buffet just waiting to be devoured, and I was more than happy to oblige.

Of course, I would get caught every time. "Ben, no!" they would shout, shooing me away from their precious snacks. "That's not for you!"

But the worst incident by far was the one with the chocolate bar that Adam and Jacob's best friend Wayne had left out. I had found it lying on a bedside table, its shiny wrapper glinting invitingly in the sunlight. I knew I wasn't supposed to have chocolate—something about it being bad for dogs—but I just couldn't resist.

I gobbled down the entire bar in two bites, wrapper, and all. It was pure bliss—for about five minutes. Then the stomach cramps hit, and I knew I was in trouble.

A frantic trip to the vet and one very unpleasant bout of induced vomiting later, I was back home, my tail firmly tucked between my legs. I had learned my lesson—chocolate was off the menu.

It was after this incident that my master decided to act. "We need to find a way to keep Ben occupied," he said to my mistress one evening. "Something that will keep him from constantly searching for food."

And that's how I ended up with the biggest, juiciest rawhide bone I had ever seen.

My master had gone to the pet store and picked out the largest bone they had—a massive thing that looked like it had come from a dinosaur. I could barely contain my excitement as he walked through the door with it, my tail wagging so hard.

"Easy there, Ben!" my master laughed, holding the bone up high. "This is for you, but you have to promise to make it last, okay?"

I barked my agreement, my eyes never leaving the prize in his hands. He set the bone down on the floor, and I pounced on it like a starving wolf.

But there was just one problem - the bone was so big, I couldn't quite fit it through the doorway to the living room. I tried turning my head this way and that, but no matter what angle I tried, the bone just wouldn't budge.

My master watched me struggle for a few minutes, a bemused smile on his face. "Need some help there, Benny?" he asked.

I looked up at him, my eyes pleading. "I've got this," I seemed to say. "Just give me a minute."

And then, inspiration struck. I carefully set the bone down on the floor and began to nudge it with my nose, turning it until it was at just the right angle. Then, with a triumphant bark, I picked it up again and marched proudly into the living room, my prize held high.

My master shook his head, laughing. "You're a clever one, aren't you, Ben?"

I just grinned around the bone in my mouth, my tail wagging happily. With a bone this size, I knew I would be occupied for hours - no more rummaging in bins or sneaking into bedrooms for me.

As I settled down on my bed, the bone clamped firmly between my paws, I couldn't help but feel a sense of contentment wash over me. Sure, my tummy might still try to control my brain from time to time, but with a family who loved me and a bone the size of a small country, I knew I could handle anything.

And who knows? Maybe next time, I'd even share my bone with May and Suki - if they asked nicely, of course.

A Day at the Seaside

The sun was shining, the birds were singing, and I, Ben the Labrador, was about to embark on my first-ever trip to the seaside. The place was called Saltburn, and I had heard my family talking about it for weeks, their voices filled with excitement.

"Ben's going to love it there," the mistress said, packing a picnic basket with all sorts of delicious-smelling treats. "The fresh sea air, the wide open spaces - it's a dog's paradise!"

I wagged my tail in agreement, my whole body wiggling with anticipation. I had no idea what the seaside was, but if my family was this excited about it, it had to be good.

The drive to Saltburn was a bit long, but I didn't mind the car. I took in all the passing sights and ignored Bronwyn's complaints of my drool as I panted in the car. I could not help myself; I was far too excited.

When we finally arrived, I couldn't wait to explore. However, the master said that the tide was in and covering the beach, so we headed to a nearby grassy area with a stream running through it. It was the perfect spot for a picnic.

The master and mistress spread out a blanket on the grass, and we all settled down to enjoy our lunch. I, of course, was more interested in the contents of the picnic basket than the scenery, but the mistress made sure to pack plenty of treats for me too.

After we had eaten our fill, Bronwyn and I wasted no time in exploring the area. She clambered over the wooden play apparatus that had been set up near the stream while I splashed around in the cool, clear water.

Bronwyn giggled as I shook myself off, sending water droplets flying everywhere. "Oh, Ben!" she laughed, covering her face with her hands. "You're getting me all wet!"

But I could tell she didn't really mind. She loved playing with me just as much as I loved playing with her.

As the afternoon wore on, the tide began to recede, revealing the wide, sandy beach. The master and mistress packed up our picnic, and we made our way down to the shore.

The beach was unlike anything I had ever seen before. The sand stretched out as far as the eye could see, and the ocean sparkled in the sunlight. I let out a joyful bark and bounded across the sand, my paws leaving deep imprints behind me.

The master pulled out a bright blue ball from his backpack and tossed it for me to chase. I bounded after it, my paws kicking up sand as I ran.

But when I caught the ball, I realised I had a bit of a problem. You see, I had never quite learned how to let go of things once I had them in my mouth. It was a habit I had developed at home, where I would often steal plastic pop bottles and make my family chase me around the house to get them back.

And now, with the ball firmly clamped between my jaws, I took off running down the beach, the master chasing after me.

"Ben!" he called, laughing and panting as he tried to keep up. "Come back here, you rascal!"

But I was having too much fun to stop. I zigzagged across the sand, my tail wagging furiously as I led the master on a merry chase.

Finally, after what felt like hours (but was probably only a few minutes), the master caught up to me and managed to pry the ball from my mouth. "You're a handful, you know that?" he said, ruffling my fur affectionately.

I just grinned up at him, my tongue lolling out of my mouth. I knew he loved me, handful or not.

As the day went on, we played and explored to our hearts' content. I chased seagulls (but never caught any), dug holes in the sand (much to the mistress's dismay), and even took a tentative dip in the ocean (which was a lot bigger and scarier than the stream, but still fun).

But perhaps the most memorable moment of the day came when the master and mistress bought Bronwyn an ice cream cone from a nearby stand. It was a hot day, and the treat was melting quickly in the sun. The sweet, creamy scent was too tempting to resist. Before anyone could stop me, I had jumped up and nudged the ice cream right out of Bronwyn's hand.

"Ben, no!" the mistress scolded, as Bronwyn let out a cry of dismay. "That was Bronwyn's ice cream!"

I hung my head, my tail tucking between my legs. I hadn't meant to upset anyone - I just couldn't control myself around food.

But the master and mistress were quick to forgive me. They bought Bronwyn a new ice cream (which she made sure to keep far away from me this time) and gave me a gentle pat on the head.

"It's okay, Ben," the master said, scratching behind my ears. "We know you didn't mean any harm. Just try to control yourself next time, okay?"

I wagged my tail in agreement, my mouth still sticky with stolen ice cream.

As the sun began to set over the sea, we packed up our things and headed back to the car. I was exhausted from all the excitement of the day, but in the best possible way.

"Did you have fun, Ben?" Bronwyn asked, giving me a sleepy cuddle in the backseat.

I licked her face in response, my tail thumping against the seat. Of course I had fun - how could I not, with a family like this?

And as I drifted off to sleep, my head resting on Bronwyn's lap, I couldn't help but feel like the luckiest dog in the world.

Because even though I may have caused a bit of mischief (okay, a lot of mischief), I knew that my family would always love me, no matter what.

And that, in my opinion, is what a day at the seaside is all about.

The Case of the Vanishing Feline

In a household as lively as ours, you'd think nothing could catch us off guard. But when May, Jacob's beloved cat and constant companion, suddenly went missing, it felt like the ground had been yanked out from under us.

It all started on a seemingly ordinary day. I was lounging in the living room, chewing on my favourite bone, when I heard Jacob calling out for May.

But May didn't come. She always came running to his call, but this time, there was only silence. Jacob's face fell as he searched the house, calling her name with increasing desperation. "May? May, where are you?"

I joined in the search, sniffing around all of May's usual hiding spots— under the bed, behind the couch, in the laundry basket. But there was no sign of her.

As the hours turned into days, the whole family became more and more worried. Jacob was beside himself. He would come home from school every day and immediately start searching the house, calling out for his beloved cat.

The master and mistress did everything they could to find May. They phoned all the local animal shelters and veterinary clinics, hoping someone had found her and brought her in. They even distributed missing cat flyers around the neighbourhood, with a picture of May and our phone number.

On our daily walks, the master would talk to everyone we passed, asking if they had seen a tabby cat. I would sniff around, hoping to catch a whiff of May's scent, but there was nothing.

We had a few false alarms where someone would call and say they had seen a cat matching May's description. The whole family would rush to the location, hearts pounding with hope, only to come back empty-handed. It was always a different cat, or no cat at all.

As the weeks went by, the house felt empty without May's presence. Suki, our other cat, would wander around aimlessly, meowing plaintively as if searching for her missing sister. Even George and Ludwig, the bearded dragons, seemed to sense that something was wrong.

But no one was more affected than Jacob. He would lie awake at night, staring at the empty spot on his bed where May used to curl up and sleep.

I would try to offer what comfort I could, but I knew that nothing could truly ease the ache of a missing loved one.

Just when we had almost given up hope, a miracle happened.

It was a typical weekday morning, and Jacob was heading out. He opened the back door, and suddenly, a familiar meow filled the air.

There, sitting on the deck, was May. She was thinner than before, her fur matted and dirty, but she was alive.

Jacob let out a cry of joy and scooped her up in his arms, tears streaming down his face. "May! Oh my god, May, you're back!"

The whole family came running at the sound of his shouts, and soon we were all gathered around May, petting her and marvelling at her return.

"Where have you been, you naughty kitty?" the mistress asked, scratching May behind the ears. "We were so worried about you!"

May just purred contentedly, rubbing her head against Jacob's chin.

I couldn't help but wonder if I had played a role in May's return. The master had never stopped looking for her on our walks, and I had always made sure to leave a little bit of my scent behind, hoping it would help guide her home.

Had May finally caught a whiff of my scent and followed it back to us? I liked to think so.

In the end, it didn't matter how or why she had come back. All that mattered was that our family was whole again.

That night, I watched as Jacob snuggled up to May, his arms wrapped tightly around her. "You are grounded," he murmured, planting a kiss on her furry head.

May just purred, her eyes closed in contentment.

The Day the Law Came Knocking

It was a quiet afternoon in the house, with just the mistress and Nana Lynda at home. The two women were sitting in the kitchen, chatting over a cup of tea, while I lay contentedly at their feet.

The peaceful atmosphere was suddenly shattered by a loud, insistent knocking on both the front and back doors. The mistress and Nana Lynda exchanged a startled glance, their conversation abruptly cut off.

"Who on earth could that be?" the mistress wondered aloud, rising from her chair.

"I have no idea," Nana Lynda replied, a note of unease in her voice.

The mistress headed towards the front door, while Nana Lynda made her way to the back. I, sensing Nana Lynda's anxiety, decided to accompany her, my tail wagging reassuringly.

As Nana Lynda opened the back door, we were confronted by two stern-faced individuals, a man and a woman, both dressed in plain clothes. They held up badges, identifying themselves as police officers.

"Good afternoon," the male officer said, his voice gruff. "We're looking for information about a youth who is alleged to live at this address." He then proceeded in describing who it was they were looking for.

Nana Lynda blinked in surprise, her hand tightening on the doorknob. "I'm sorry, but there's no one here by that description," she said, her voice trembling slightly.

The officers exchanged a glance, their expressions sceptical. "Mind if we take a look around?" the female officer asked, already stepping past Nana Lynda and into the house.

I couldn't help but let out a few warning barks, my protective instincts kicking in. Who were these strangers, barging into our home uninvited?

The officers paid me no mind, moving swiftly through the kitchen and out into the garden, as if expecting to find someone hiding there.

Meanwhile, at the front door, the mistress was having a similar conversation with another pair of officers. They demanded to see identification, which the mistress provided with a sense of growing frustration.

"I'm telling you, there's no one here by that name," she insisted, her voice taking on an edge of annoyance. "You've got the wrong house."

The officers studied her ID carefully, comparing it to the information they had on file. Finally, with a curt nod, they handed it back to her.

"Apologies for the intrusion," one of the officers said, not sounding particularly apologetic. "We had reason to believe the individual we're looking for might be connected to this address, but it appears our information was incorrect."

The mistress nodded, her lips pressed together in a thin line. "I appreciate you doing your job," she said, her tone making it clear that she didn't appreciate it at all, "but I'd like to know why you thought this man would be here?"

The officers refused to answer the question. With a final apology, they turned and left, their footsteps echoing down the front path.

In the kitchen, the other pair of officers had finished their search of the garden and were making their way back inside. Nana Lynda was looking pale and shaken, her hands trembling as she gripped the back of a chair for support.

I nuzzled against her leg, offering what comfort I could. I didn't like seeing Nana Lynda upset, and I could tell that the unexpected visit from the police had really rattled her.

The mistress came into the kitchen, her face flushed with anger. "The nerve of them," she muttered, shaking her head. "Barging in here like that, without so much as a by-your-leave."

Nana Lynda nodded, taking a deep breath to steady herself. "It was quite frightening," she admitted, reaching down to give me a grateful pat. "But I'm glad Ben was here with me. He's such a comfort."

I wagged my tail, my chest swelling with pride. It was my job to protect my family, and I took that responsibility very seriously.

As the officers left, the mistress and Nana Lynda slowly began to relax, the tension draining from their bodies. They looked at each other, and suddenly, they both burst out laughing.

"Oh my goodness," the mistress giggled, wiping tears of mirth from her eyes. "Can you imagine if they had found someone hiding here? I wonder what he's allegedly done to have that many police officers searching for him?"

Nana Lynda chuckled, shaking her head. "Who knows, but I don't think my poor heart could have taken that," she said, still laughing. "What a story to tell the boys when they get home!"

I watched my two favourite ladies, my tail thumping happily against the floor. I may not have understood everything that had just happened, but I knew one thing for sure—I would always be there to protect my family, no matter what. Even if it was just from a case of mistaken identity and some overzealous police officers.

As the laughter died down and the kettle was put on for a fresh cup of tea, I settled back down at their feet, content in the knowledge that all was well in our little corner of the world. And if anyone tried to disrupt that peace again, well . . . they'd have to go through me first.

The Tyrannical Landlord

Life in our household had been relatively peaceful since our brush with the law. However, little did I know that our tranquil existence was about to be disrupted by a man named Harry Peters.

It all started with a letter from Patterson Estate agents. I was lounging at the mistress's feet as she opened the envelope, her brow furrowing as she read the contents.

"That's odd," she murmured, handing the letter to the master. "They say that the landlord, Harry Peters, is offering to fund our deposit and arrange a mortgage if we want to buy this house from him."

The master scanned the letter, his expression equally puzzled. "Why would he do that? We've never even met the man."

The mistress shrugged, tapping her fingers against the kitchen table. "I don't know, but something about it feels off. Maybe we should talk to my Dad about it."

I perked up my ears at the mention of the mistress's father. He was a wise old man who always had good advice to give.

Later that evening, the mistress's father came over for tea. As they sat around the table, the master brought up the letter from the estate agents.

"Harry Peters?" the mistress's father said, his eyebrows shooting up. "I've heard that name before. Hang on a minute."

He pulled out his phone and did a quick search. When he showed the screen to the mistress and master, their faces went pale.

"Drug dealing? Assault?" the mistress whispered, her voice trembling. "We're renting from a criminal?"

The master shook his head, his jaw clenched. "No wonder we were never approved for credit. The address must be blacklisted."

I didn't understand everything they were saying, but I could sense the tension in the room. My tail stopped wagging, and I pressed myself closer to the mistress's legs, offering what comfort I could.

In the end, the mistress and master decided to turn down the landlord's offer. They didn't want to be involved with someone who had such a shady past.

But our troubles were far from over.

A few weeks later, I was out in the garden, enjoying the sunshine, when I heard a car pull up in the driveway. I trotted over to investigate and saw a man getting out of the vehicle - a man I had never seen before.

He was tall and broad-shouldered, with a face that looked like it had been carved from granite. His eyes were cold and hard, and I immediately felt my hackles rise.

The man strode up to the front door and knocked loudly. The mistress answered, her face going pale when he announced his name.

"Harry Peters," the man said, his voice like gravel. "I'm your landlord."

The mistress swallowed hard, her hand tightening on the doorknob. "What can I do for you, Mr. Peters?"

The landlord pushed past her and into the house, his eyes roving over the interior. "I'm here to discuss some changes I want to make to the property."

Over the next hour, the landlord laid out his plans. He wanted to use the spare land at the back of the property to build another house, cutting down the size of our garden and fencing it off. He also wanted to build an extension to the dormer bungalow, and as a sweetener said that he would add an ensuite bathroom for Nana Lynda who had a downstairs bedroom. He also agreed to add a shower to the upstairs bathroom.

The mistress and master listened in stunned silence, their faces growing more and more troubled with each passing minute. Finally, the master spoke up.

"And what about the disruption to our lives?" he asked. "The noise, the mess, the inconvenience?"

The landlord waved a dismissive hand. "You'll be compensated for any inconvenience. And think of it this way - you'll have a nicer place to live when it's all done."

The mistress and master exchanged a glance, and I could see the resignation in their eyes. They knew they didn't have much choice in the matter.

Over the next few months, our lives were turned upside down by the construction work. Builders tramped in and out of the house at all hours, hammering and drilling and making a terrible racket. I spent most of my time hiding under the table, my paws over my ears.

When the work was finally finished, Adam moved into a downstairs bedroom, giving him some much-needed privacy. The mistress and master were relieved that the disruption was over, but they couldn't shake the feeling that something wasn't quite right.

Their suspicions were confirmed when the landlord came to visit again. This time, he had a new offer for them.

"I own another property just down the road," he said, his eyes glinting with something I couldn't quite identify. "It's a real nice place, but I am moving out. I want you to come and take a look at it, see if you are interested in renting it whilst the development work is being carried out on this one."

The mistress and master were hesitant, but they agreed to go and view the house. When they came back, their faces were grim.

"It's a lovely house," the mistress said, her voice tight. "But there's a catch. The landlord wants to retain a bedroom for himself and keep it always locked. No explanation given."

Nana Lynda's eyes widened. "What on earth for?"

The master shook his head. "Given his reputation, I think we can all guess. Drugs, most likely. And we want no part of it."

"I wonder if he was the reason we had the visit from the police? What if it was one of his dealers they were looking for?" said the mistress.

I felt a growl rumble in my throat. I didn't like this landlord one bit. He was trouble, and I could sense it in my bones.

Ghostly Encounters

With two mischievous cats, two bearded dragons, and one perpetually hungry Labrador (that's me, by the way) naturally there would be periods of chaos. But since the landlord had built the extension, things had taken a turn for the downright spooky.

It all started with the chairs in the kitchen. One minute, they would be sitting innocently at the table, and the next, they would suddenly tip over, as if pushed by an invisible hand. The first time it happened, I nearly jumped out of my fur, convinced that we were under attack by some unseen force.

But that was just the beginning. Soon, strange orbs started zooming through the house. I would chase after them, barking furiously, but they moved too quickly and always seemed to vanish just as I got close.

Even more unsettling was the cold spot in the mistress and master's bedroom. No matter how high they cranked up the heat, that one area of the room always felt like a walk-in freezer. I would avoid it at all costs, my tail tucked firmly between my legs.

The mistress, I knew, was spiritually gifted. She wasn't entirely surprised by the ghostly activity. She confirmed to the master that she had sensed an increasing level of spirits in the house, and where previously this would not have bothered her, even she was feeling the toll of the constant paranormal occurrences.

"I'm so tired of things going wrong in this house," she sighed, rubbing her temples. "Since the arrival of Harry and all the building work, the energy in here has changed. It's oppressive. Have you noticed? Even the kids seem unhappy and in a mood all the time. You and your mum snap at each other. It's not right."

The master nodded in agreement, his brow furrowed with concern. "We need to do something about this. It's getting out of hand. It will get even worse when he starts the development work. That's if he gets the planning permission through."

Adam, too, was feeling the effects of our ghostly visitors. He would often come to breakfast looking like he hadn't slept a wink, complaining about being woken up in the middle of the night by strange noises and sensations.

"I'll invite the spooky team over, see if they can help," said the mistress.

The spooky team comprised a group of seemingly ordinary women of various ages. They arrived within a few days of the mistress's phone call. All were friendly and gave me lots of ear scratches and belly tickles. Like the mistress, they too appeared to have a close affinity with animals. I could also see that they regarded the mistress very highly and with a deep, unwavering respect.

I, of course, was not allowed in the mistress's room when the time came for them to proceed with the task at hand, but I waited outside the door. I wanted to remain close to the mistress in the event she needed me.

I could hear various grunts and moans coming from the room, and my mistress and another woman calling out instructions to the others. Although their voices were serious, they did not sound as though they were in any danger. Reassured, I laid my head on my front paws and rested my eyes. It was late into the night when they finally surfaced from the room, and with hugs and laughter they left the house. As soon as the coast was clear, I went to investigate the room, and indeed the rest of the house. It did feel lighter somehow.

I listened as the mistress explained to the master that they had rescued some spirits, including the one who had been disturbing Adam, but she said that each of the team had commented about there being a vortex in their bedroom.

"What does that mean?" the master asked, his voice laced with concern.

"More spooks likely visiting," she said wearily. "I'm not sure we can stay here. With everything that has happened, the landlord too..."

"Well, all we can do is see if things get better and calm down for a bit," the master replied, trying to sound optimistic.

But as the days turned into weeks, the ghostly occurrences in our house became more and more frequent. It wasn't the kind of dramatic poltergeist activity you see in movies, but rather a constant series of small, unsettling events that slowly chipped away at our sense of peace and security.

Doors would close without any discernible wind, leaving us all feeling slightly uneasy. Lights would flicker and bulbs would burn out at an alarming rate, casting eerie shadows on the walls. And it seemed like every day, something in the house would break or fall apart, as if the very structure of our home was rebelling against us.

I remember the day the master's newly acquired fish tank sprang a leak when they tried to fill it. Water poured out onto the floor, sending the poor fish flapping and gasping for air. It took hours to clean up the mess and find a temporary home for the aquatic creatures.

Another time, the mistress opened a window to let in some fresh air, only to have the entire frame fall out. She stood there in shock, staring at the gaping hole in the wall, as if trying to comprehend how such a thing could happen.

Even the cupboard doors weren't safe, often coming off their hinges at the slightest touch. It got to the point where we were afraid to open them, never knowing what might come tumbling out.

But perhaps the most disturbing development was the horrible smell that started emanating from the drains. It was a sickening odour that would waft up from the pipes and permeate the entire house. No amount of cleaning or plunging seemed to make a difference, and we were left gagging and retching every time we entered the bathroom. When the mistress reported it to the estate agents, they sent somcone around to clear the drains, and the contractor accused my family of flushing baby wipes down the toilet. The mistress told him angrily that her children had been out of nappies for quite some time and they did not have any baby wipes in the house.

All these constant disruptions and malfunctions took a toll on my family. Tempers began to flare as nerves were frayed, and arguments would break out over the smallest things. The once happy and harmonious household was slowly descending into chaos, and even I could feel the tension in the air.

The mistress and master tried to keep a brave face for the children, but I could see the strain in their eyes. They were at their wits' end, constantly dealing with repairs and replacements, never knowing what would break down next. The mistress told the master that the latest repair she had requested was met with some animosity by the landlord and the estate agents. The master said he felt our home was turning into the 'Money Pit' and that he empathised with Tom Hanks.

I took it upon myself to keep a watchful eye on the children, especially Adam. I would sleep close to his room every night, ready to chase away any malevolent spirits that might try to disturb his slumber. And during the day, I would follow the mistress around the house, my tail wagging reassuringly, letting her know that she was never alone.

Despite my best efforts, however, the ghostly activity continued to escalate. The mistress and master grew more and more weary, their faces etched with lines of worry and exhaustion. Nana Lynda too was becoming increasingly anxious and developed this nervous cough that had me raise and prick my ears up in concern.

Finally, after a particularly trying week, the mistress broke down in tears. "I can't do this anymore," she sobbed, burying her face in her hands. "There is so much negativity here. We need to get away."

The master wrapped his arms around her, his own eyes glistening with unshed tears. "I know, love. I think it's time we started looking for a new place to live."

It was a difficult decision, but one that we all knew was necessary. It was clear that something about our home was deeply wrong, and it was affecting us in ways we couldn't even fully comprehend.

Over the next few weeks, we began the process of packing up our belongings and searching for a new place to call home. There was a sense of relief in knowing that we were escaping the oppressive atmosphere of the house.

Through it all, I did my best to offer comfort and support to my family. I would lie at their feet as they sorted through boxes, my tail thumping reassuringly against the floor. I would bring them my favourite toys, hoping to coax a smile or a laugh from their weary faces.

And when the day finally came to leave, I was right there by their side, ready to face whatever challenges lay ahead. With the love and strength of our family, I knew that we could weather any storm. Even if that storm came in the form of flickering lights, falling picture frames, and the occasional ghostly orb.

A New Home, A New Adventure

The move to our new house on Belford Road was a bittersweet experience. On one hand, I was excited to explore a new place and mark my territory. On the other hand, I could sense the stress and worry emanating from my beloved family.

The living room in our new home was much smaller than our previous one, and I could tell that the mistress and master were struggling to make ends meet. They had cleaned our old house from top to bottom, even getting the carpets professionally cleaned, but the previous landlord, Harry Peters, had refused to return their full bond.

I overheard the mistress talking to the master one evening, her voice tight with concern. "I've been getting these nasty emails from the estate agents," she said, wringing her hands. "I'm worried about what the landlord might do, given his reputation. I hope he doesn't know our new address."

The master sighed, running a hand through his hair. "The estate agents are offering to return fifty percent of the bond, and the way the email is phrased, it's clear the landlord isn't happy. It seems like this is his only and final offer."

The mistress bit her lip, her eyes filled with worry. "Let's just take it. The money isn't worth the risk of a broken leg or worse."

In the end, they did receive the partial bond, and thankfully, the landlord left them alone. But our troubles were far from over.

Our new landlord was a penny-pinching miser who refused to do any repairs or maintenance on the property. The kitchen was in dire need of some work, and the mistress's dad had to step in to help fix things up.

To make matters worse, Adam and Jacob were back to sharing a bedroom, much to their dismay. I could hear them bickering late into the night.

But there were some silver linings to our new home. The boys were still within walking distance of their schools, which made the morning routine a bit easier. And Bronwyn was able to play outside on the street, which was much safer than our old neighbourhood.

One day, Adam and Bronwyn decided to take me for a walk. I was always eager for a good stroll, and I trotted happily by their side as we made our way down the street.

Suddenly, we came across a couple walking a Husky puppy. The little thing was adorable, with fluffy white fur and bright blue eyes. As an older dog, I felt the need to establish my dominance and teach the puppy some manners. So, I gave it a quick nip on the ear, a common way for adult dogs to assert their authority and teach puppies proper behaviour.

But the puppy's owners didn't see it that way. The man started yelling at Adam, his face turning red with anger. "Keep your dog under control!" he shouted, jabbing a finger at me.

Adam, being the protective brother he was, immediately jumped to my defence. "He was just teaching the puppy some manners!" he yelled back, his grip tightening on my leash. "Your puppy is fine!"

The argument quickly escalated, with both parties shouting and gesticulating wildly. I cowered behind Adam's legs, my tail tucked between my legs. I hadn't meant to cause any trouble.

"Get Mam," Adam said.

Bronwyn ran back home to fetch the mistress. She came running towards us, just as Adam and the man had now squared up to each other. The mistress quickly positioned herself between Adam and the man, holding up her hands in a placating gesture.

"Whoa, whoa, whoa," she said, her voice calm but firm. "Let's all take a deep breath here. I'm sure we can resolve this amicably."

She turned to Bronwyn, her expression serious. "Please take Ben back to the house. I'll handle this."

Bronwyn nodded, grabbing my leash from Adam, and leading me away. I glanced back over my shoulder, whining softly. I didn't want to leave Adam and the mistress alone with that angry man.

As we approached the house, Nana Lynda came marching out, her face set with determination. She had seen the commotion from the window and was prepared to give the man a piece of her mind. However, she met the mistress now walking back up the street with Adam, who looked visibly upset.

Nana Lynda's expression softened as she took in the sight of her grandson. "What happened, love?" she asked.

The mistress explained the situation, and Nana Lynda shook her head in disbelief. "Some people just don't understand dog behaviour," she said, giving me a comforting pat on the head.

To everyone's surprise, the man came to our house later that day and apologised profusely for his behaviour. He admitted that he had overreacted and that he was sorry for causing such a scene.

From that day forward, the couple was much nicer to us, and their daughter even became good friends with Bronwyn. They would often play together on the street, giggling and chasing each other around.

As for me, I learned that not everyone understands the ways of dogs, and that sometimes, my instincts can get me into trouble. I vowed to be more careful in the future, especially around unfamiliar puppies and their protective owners.

A Fiery Tail

As the winter nights drew in, I found myself spending more and more time indoors with my beloved family. One of the advantages of our new home on Belford Road was that it seemed to warm up much quicker than our previous place. The mistress would often light the fire in the living room, creating a cosy atmosphere that I couldn't resist.

On one particularly chilly evening, the mistress and Bronwyn were relaxing on the couch, enjoying the warmth of the crackling fire. The master was in the kitchen, busy preparing our evening meal. The delicious smells wafting from the stove made my stomach grumble with anticipation.

I, on the other hand, had managed to sneak into the boys' bedroom and snatch a plastic bottle from their stash. It was one of my favourite toys, and I loved nothing more than playing with it, wagging my tail furiously as I pranced around the living room.

Little did I know that my enthusiastic tail-wagging would soon lead to a bit of a crisis.

As I played with the bottle, I inadvertently backed up too close to the fire. Suddenly, I heard the mistress cry out in alarm.

"Ben! Your tail!" she shouted, leaping up from the couch.

Bronwyn was hot on her heels, her eyes wide with worry. "His tail is on fire!"

I didn't understand what all the fuss was about. I thought they were just excited to play with me, so I wagged my tail even harder.

The mistress and Bronwyn were frantically trying to catch me, but I thought it was all a big game. I darted and dodged, my tail still wagging merrily, oblivious to the fact that it was now sporting a small flame.

In my excitement, I accidentally knocked a coal out of the fire. It landed on the carpet, and the mistress quickly rushed to pick it up before it could cause any damage.

"Oh no!" she exclaimed. "It's already burned a hole in the carpet!"

Meanwhile, Bronwyn had finally managed to catch up to me. She quickly grabbed a glass of water from the coffee table and doused my tail, extinguishing the flame.

I yelped in surprise, not understanding why she had done that. I wasn't hurt, but I was a bit confused by all the commotion.

The mistress and Bronwyn checked me over thoroughly, making sure that I hadn't been injured. They were relieved to find that my thick fur had protected me from any serious harm.

"Thank goodness he's okay," the mistress said, giving me a big hug. "But we can't let this happen again. We need to get a fire guard to keep him away from the flames."

Bronwyn nodded in agreement. "Maybe we should also keep a closer eye on him when he's playing. You know how he loves to get into mischief."

I just wagged my tail, happy to be the centre of attention. I had no idea that I had come close to a dangerous situation. In my mind, it had all been a fun game.

The master, hearing the commotion, came in from the kitchen. "What's going on in here?" he asked, taking in the scene of the burned carpet and the slightly damp but otherwise unharmed Labrador.

The mistress explained what had happened, and the master shook his head in disbelief. "Oh, Ben," he chuckled. "You do keep us on our toes."

From that day forward, the mistress made sure to keep a fire guard in front of the fireplace whenever it was lit. She also kept a closer eye on me when I was playing, making sure that I didn't get into any more mischief.

The Mouse House Escapade

It was just another ordinary day in my life as Ben, the loyal and energetic dog of the household. I was lounging on my favourite spot in the living room when suddenly, I heard a commotion that made my ears perk up. The cats, usually calm and composed, were now frantically running around the house, their meows echoing through the hall.

"Meow! Meow! There's a mouse in the house!" I heard them cry out.

Curious and excited, I jumped up and started barking, my tail wagging with anticipation. "Woof! Woof! Let me join the chase!" I exclaimed, eager to be a part of the action.

The cats darted from room to room, their paws plucking the carpets furiously as they tried to corner the elusive mouse. I followed close behind, my nose to the ground, trying to catch a whiff of the intruder.

"I think it went into the conservatory!" one of the cats yelled, and we all rushed towards the glass-enclosed room.

The mistress, always kind and compassionate, couldn't bear the thought of any harm coming to the little creature. "Adam, help, but don't hurt it!" she called out to her son.

Adam, quick on his feet, managed to corner and grab the mouse, but it wriggled free from his grasp and scurried up his hooded top. "Oh no! It's in my clothes!" he yelped, dancing around trying to shake the mouse loose.

The mistress and Bronwyn, rushed to Adam's aid, their hands frantically trying to locate the mouse. "Hold still, Adam! We'll get it out!" Bronwyn reassured him. They were all laughing so hard, to the point of tears.

I watched in amusement, my tail still wagging, as the humans worked together to contain the mischievous mouse. After a few minutes of chaos, they finally managed to trap it in a box.

"Phew!" the mistress sighed, wiping her brow. "But we can't keep the mouse here. It might find its way back into the house."

Bronwyn nodded in agreement. "I think we should take Ben for a walk to the park and release the mouse there. It'll be far enough away from the house."

My ears perked up at the mention of a walk, and I barked excitedly. "Woof! Woof! Yes, let's go to the park!"

The mistress and Bronwyn gathered my leash and the box containing the mouse, and we set off for the local park. The sun was shining, and the breeze carried the scent of freshly cut grass. I trotted happily beside my humans, my nose exploring all the new smells.

When we reached the park, Bronwyn carefully opened the box and released the mouse near a cluster of bushes. "There you go, little one. You're free now," she said softly.

I watched as the mouse scampered away, disappearing into the foliage. "Goodbye, mouse! Thanks for the exciting day!" I barked, my tail wagging as I bid farewell to our tiny visitor.

As we walked back home, I knew that life with my loving family would never be dull, and I looked forward to many more memorable moments together.

A Startling Discovery

I was lounging on the landing in my favourite spot, enjoying the warm sunlight streaming through the window, when I suddenly felt an odd sensation coursing through my body. Not knowing what was wrong, I moved to the stairs to go and find Bronwyn, who was home from school. Before I knew it, I found myself tumbling down the stairs, my paws flailing as I tried to regain my balance.

I landed at the bottom with a thud, momentarily stunned. Jacob, one of the boys, rushed from the kitchen where he had been preparing a snack and to my side. He gently helped me to my feet and checked me over, his hands running through my fur, looking for any signs of injury. Thankfully, I seemed to be okay, just a little shaken up.

Jacob called out to Bronwyn, who quickly dialled the mistress at work to inform her about my unexpected tumble. I could hear Bronwyn explaining the situation over the phone, and Jacob reassuring the mistress that I was fine now, but they weren't sure what had caused me to fall down the stairs.

Later that evening, after my usual walk, I settled onto my bed in the kitchen, ready to drift off to sleep. Suddenly, that strange feeling returned, and an overwhelming sense of unease washed over me. Instinctively, I ran to find my mistress, seeking comfort and reassurance.

As I reached her, my body betrayed me, and I collapsed to the floor, my limbs jerking uncontrollably. I could hear the mistress's panicked voice as she called out to the master. "It looks like he's having some sort of seizure," she said as she gently stroked my fur and whispered soothing words. The sensation stopped, and although wobbly, I rose from the floor, shook myself off and wagged my tail to let them know I was okay.

"I'll ring the vet's in the morning," my master confirmed.

Thankfully, the rest of the night passed without further incident.

The following day I was bundled into the car and taken to the vet. At the veterinary clinic, the vet examined me thoroughly, asking the mistress and master about my symptoms and behaviour. After running some tests, the vet delivered the diagnosis: epilepsy.

The vet explained that epilepsy is a neurological disorder characterised by recurrent seizures. These seizures occur when there is abnormal electrical activity in the brain, causing involuntary muscle contractions, loss of consciousness, and other neurological signs. Epilepsy can be inherited from parents, but it can also be caused by various factors such as brain tumours, infections, toxins, or head injuries.

The vet reassured the mistress and master that epilepsy in dogs can often be managed with proper care and medication. She provided advice on how to keep me safe during a seizure, such as moving furniture away to prevent injury and staying calm, as dogs can sense their owners' anxiety.

The vet also prescribed medication to be administered if my seizures lasted longer than a couple of minutes, which could help bring me out of the episode more quickly. They emphasised the importance of keeping a seizure diary to track the frequency, duration, and any potential triggers of my seizures, which would help in monitoring my condition and adjusting my treatment plan if needed.

As we drove home, I could sense the mistress and master's concern and love for me. They gently stroked my fur, whispering words of comfort and reassurance. I knew that, no matter what, I had a family who would be there for me every step of the way.

Living with epilepsy would undoubtedly bring some changes to our lives, but I was determined not to let it define me. I was still Ben, the loyal and loving dog who brought joy to my family's lives. With their support and the guidance of the vet, I knew we would find a way to manage this new reality together.

A Picnic Mishap

The sun was shining brightly as the mistress and master took me to the park for my daily walk. I couldn't contain my excitement, my tail wagging furiously as we set off down the familiar streets, eager to explore the lush green field and breathe in the fresh air.

As soon as we reached the grassy expanse, the master unclipped my leash, and I was free to run to my heart's content. I darted across the field, chasing butterflies and revelling in the feeling of the soft grass beneath my paws.

Suddenly, an enticing aroma caught my attention. My nose twitched as I followed the scent, my stomach growling in anticipation. As I drew closer, I spotted a couple sitting on a picnic blanket, enjoying what appeared to be a delicious meal of fish and chips.

The temptation was too great to resist. Controlled by my insatiable appetite, I made a beeline for their picnic, my eyes locked on the tantalising food. The couple, startled by my sudden appearance, tried to shoo me away, but I was determined.

"Oh my goodness!" the woman exclaimed as I dove into their meal, gobbling up the fish and chips with gusto.

"Ben! No!" I heard the master shout, but it was too late. I had already devoured most of their food, including the wooden fork that had been resting on the tray.

The couple looked at me with a mix of shock and annoyance. "I can't believe this!" the man said, throwing his hands up in exasperation.

The master, embarrassed by my behaviour, quickly approached the couple, apologising profusely. "I'm so sorry about this. Ben is usually better behaved. Please, let me buy you another portion of fish and chips to make up for it."

The couple hesitated for a moment before agreeing, and the master hurried off to the nearby fish and chip shop to replace their ruined meal. Meanwhile, the mistress scolded me, her voice stern. "Ben, that was very naughty. You know better than to steal other people's food."

I hung my head, feeling guilty for my actions, but the lingering taste of the fish and chips still danced on my tongue. The master returned with a fresh portion for the couple, apologising once more before we headed home.

That evening, as punishment for my misbehaviour, the master decided not to give me my usual dinner. I whined and pawed at my empty bowl, but deep down, I knew I deserved it. Little did they know that it was probably for the best, as later that night, I began to feel sick to my stomach.

I retreated to a quiet corner of the house, and before long, I started retching. To my surprise, up came the wooden fork I had ingested earlier, along with the remnants of the ill-gotten fish and chips. The mistress and master looked on with concern, but thankfully, after expelling the foreign object, I started to feel better.

The next morning, I woke up feeling like my old self again. The mistress, taking pity on me, gave me my breakfast as usual. As I munched on my kibble, I couldn't help but reflect on the previous day's events. While I felt guilty for ruining the couple's picnic and causing trouble for my family, I had to admit that the fish and chips had been delicious.

Looking up at the mistress with my best puppy dog eyes, I silently vowed to try and control my impulses in the future. I knew that my family loved me unconditionally, but I also realised that it was important to respect others and their belongings.

As the mistress patted my head affectionately, I leaned into her touch, grateful for her forgiveness and understanding. I knew that I was a lucky dog to have such a wonderful family, and I promised myself that I would do my best to be a good boy from now on . . . or at least, I would try my hardest to resist the temptation of unguarded picnics in the park.

A New Home for the Holidays

Life in our cosy little house was changing, and I could sense it in the air. Nana Lynda, one of the older members of our pack, had decided it was time for her to venture out on her own. She packed her belongings and moved into her own flat, leaving behind a void that we all felt.

The mistress grew restless, pacing around the house and complaining about the lack of space. "This house is just too small!" she would exclaim, her voice filled with frustration. "I can't even move the furniture around in these tiny rooms!"

She tried to rearrange the furniture, hoping to create a sense of openness, but it was an impossible task. The rooms were simply too small to accommodate any significant changes. Even when she opened the windows, the energy in the rooms remained stagnant. Adam and Jacob, growing bigger by the day, needed their own spaces to call their own.

Determined to find a solution, the mistress set out on a mission to find a new home for our family. She spent days searching the internet, until finally, she announced with a sparkle in her eye, "I've found it!" Her voice brimmed with excitement. "The perfect house for us. We have to view it."

The master, always supportive of the mistress's decisions, agreed to go and view the house with her. They returned later that day, their faces a mix of excitement and apprehension.

"The house is perfect," the mistress said, "but the timing is a bit tricky. We'll have to move in on the second of January."

I tilted my head, wondering what that meant for our holiday celebrations. As it turned out, it meant that our Christmas would be unlike any other.

The weeks leading up to the move were a flurry of activity. The mistress and the master were busy packing, trying to navigate around all of us animals. The cats, usually aloof and independent, seemed to sense the impending change and stuck close to the family, often curling up in the boxes as if claiming them as their new homes.

I tried my best to stay out of the way, but my curiosity often got the better of me. I would sniff the boxes, wagging my tail as I discovered familiar scents mixed with the smell of cardboard and packing tape. The mistress would gently shoo me away, reminding me that there would be plenty of time to explore once we were in our new home.

On Christmas Day, instead of the usual festive decorations and the aroma of a delicious feast, our home was filled with cardboard boxes and the sound of packing tape being stretched and torn. The family ate their Christmas dinners on lap trays, surrounded by the chaos of the impending move.

I watched as they packed away our memories, carefully wrapping fragile items and labelling boxes with their contents. The boys seemed excited about the prospect of having their own rooms, but I could sense a hint of nostalgia in the air as we prepared to leave the place we had called home.

As the New Year approached, the house was nearly empty, echoing with the ghosts of laughter and love that had once filled its walls. On the morning of the big move, I hopped into the car, ready to embark on a new adventure with my beloved family. The cats were safely tucked away in their carriers, meowing their displeasure at the disruption to their routine.

The journey to our new home was filled with anticipation and a touch of nervousness. When we arrived, I bounded out of the car, eager to explore our new surroundings. The mistress and the master busied themselves with unloading boxes and directing family members who had come to help. Adam, Jacob, and Bronwyn raced off to claim their new rooms.

As I wandered through the house, sniffing every corner and investigating every nook and cranny, I couldn't help but feel a sense of excitement. The cats, released from their carriers, cautiously explored their new domain, their tails twitching with curiosity.

This was our third home together, and I knew that if I had my family by my side, any place could feel like home. The mistress, finally able to arrange the furniture to her liking, seemed to breathe a sigh of relief, her frustrations melting away as she settled into our new space.

That night, as we all lay in our new beds, exhausted from the day's events, I curled up at the foot of my mistress's bed, my tail wagging contentedly. The cats, having found their favourite spots, purred softly in the distance.

Ember, the Black Cat

Life in our forever home was always full of surprises, and the latest addition to our family was no exception. The mistress had been longing for a black cat for some time, and when she heard about a young black feline who needed a loving home, she knew it was meant to be. The mistress named her Ember.

Ember's story was a touching one. At just eighteen months old, she had already given birth to two kittens, her previous owner having failed to get Ember spayed.

The mistress, with her compassionate heart, understood that the kittens would likely find homes more easily than their mother. So, she decided to welcome Ember into our family, giving her a chance at a better life.

When Ember first arrived, I was excited to have a new playmate. However, I quickly realised that she was not accustomed to living with dogs. Whenever I approached her, she would hiss and swat at me with her sharp claws. "Stay away from me, you big oaf!" she seemed to say, her eyes narrowed in suspicion.

I tried my best to give Ember her space, but my curiosity and desire to be friends often got the better of me. "Come on, Ember!" I would bark, wagging my tail. "Let's play together!"

But she would simply turn her back on me and saunter away, her tail held high in the air.

Over time, Ember began to tolerate my presence, but she made it clear that she had no intention of entertaining me. She preferred to keep to herself, finding solace in the quiet corners of the house. The mistress, however, formed a special bond with Ember, and the two became inseparable.

The family couldn't help but laugh at Ember's peculiar antics. Instead of playing with the fancy cat toys the mistress had bought for her, Ember found endless amusement in a simple pair of socks. She would toss them in the air, pouncing and kicking at them with her hind paws. "Look at me!" she seemed to say, her eyes sparkling with mischief. "Who needs expensive toys when you have socks?"

But Ember's most unusual quirk was her fascination with the mistress's hair. Every time the mistress washed her hair, Ember would be right there, waiting to lick it. "What are you doing, Ember?" the mistress would giggle as the cat's rough tongue raked through her damp locks.

I watched in bewilderment as Ember groomed the mistress's hair, purring contentedly. It was as if she was claiming the mistress as her own, making sure everyone knew who she belonged to.

Despite Ember's indifference towards me, I couldn't help but admire her independent spirit and the joy she brought to the family. The laughter she inspired with her quirky behaviour filled our home with warmth and happiness.

As time passed, Ember and I learned to coexist peacefully.

While we may never have been the best of friends, we found a way to share our forever home and the love of our family. I realised that sometimes, the most unexpected friendships can form under the same roof, even if they look a little different from what we imagine.

Ember's presence in our lives was a reminder that love comes in many forms, and that there is always room in our hearts for one more. As I watched her curl up on the mistress's lap, purring contentedly, I knew that she had found her true home with us, just as I had. Together, we were a family, bound by the love and laughter that filled our days, and I couldn't have been happier to share this forever home with all of them.

A Farewell to a Scaly Friend

The day started like any other, with the usual bustling activity. However, there was a noticeable absence: the mistress had gone on an overnight work trip, leaving the rest of us to hold down the fort. Little did we know that this day would bring a profound loss to our family.

I first sensed that something was amiss when I noticed the master's subdued demeanour. He moved about the house with a heaviness in his steps, his brow furrowed with concern. Curiosity piqued, I followed him to the room where George and Ludwig, our beloved bearded dragons, resided

As I entered the room, I was struck by the eerie stillness. The usual hum of George's heat lamp was absent, and the vivarium that had once been his domain now seemed lifeless. Below George's enclosure, Ludwig, our larger bearded dragon, stirred in his own vivarium. He seemed to sense the change in the atmosphere, his head tilted as if questioning the sudden quietude.

The master gently reached into George's enclosure, his hands trembling slightly as he lifted George's motionless body. I watched, my tail drooping, as the master cradled George in his palms, tears welling up in his eyes. It was then that I realised the terrible truth: George, our scaly companion, had passed away.

Ludwig, perhaps sensing the master's distress, began to pace in his vivarium. It was as if he, too, understood the gravity of the loss that had befallen our family.

My heart ached for the master and the mistress, knowing how much George had meant to them. The mistress had developed a special bond with the bearded dragon, often wearing him as a unique accessory. She delighted in the surprised expressions of visitors as George perched contentedly on her shoulder, his scales glistening in the sunlight.

Despite his sickly nature, having never fully recovered from his rescue, George had captured the hearts of our entire family. As the day wore on, a sombre mood settled over the house. The master, not wanting to disrupt the mistress's work trip, chose to wait until her return to share the heartbreaking news. I could sense his internal struggle, torn between his desire to be honest and his wish to protect her from the pain of loss.

When the mistress finally returned home, the master greeted her with a tight embrace. I watched as realisation dawned on her face, her smile fading as she understood the gravity of the situation. The master gently led her to the room where George had once resided, and together, they mourned the loss of their cherished companion.

Ludwig, still restless in his vivarium, seemed to mirror the family's grief. His usually voracious appetite had diminished, and he spent more time basking under his heat lamp, as if seeking solace in its warmth.

The mistress decided to bury George in the front garden under her favourite magnolia bush, the master and Bronwyn helping her to say goodbye.

As the days passed, the pain of George's absence gradually began to heal, replaced by the warmth of cherished memories. The family found solace in the knowledge that they had provided George with a loving home, filled with care and affection, until his final moments. Ludwig, too, seemed to gradually return to his usual self, perhaps finding comfort in the familiar routines and the love of the family.

Through the tears and the heartache, I realised that the love we shared as a family extended beyond the boundaries of species. George, in his own unique way, had taught us the value of embracing the unexpected and finding joy in the simplest of things.

As I lay my head on the mistress's lap, offering her the comfort of my presence, I knew that George's memory would forever be etched in our hearts. He may have been a small, scaly creature, but his impact on our lives had been immeasurable. And though he was gone, his spirit would live on, forever a part of our home, alongside Ludwig, who would serve as a living reminder of the love we had shared with George.

The Iced Bun Heist

The irresistible aroma of freshly baked goods wafted through the house, making my mouth water in eager anticipation. Jacob had arrived home from school carrying a delightful prize—a plate of plump, glistening iced finger buns he'd made in his home economics class.

"These are for our teatime treat!" Jacob announced proudly as he arranged the sugary buns on the plate with care.

I watched with rapt longing as he fussed over their presentation. Each one had a velvety sheen of vanilla icing that seemed to glisten under the kitchen lights. The soft, buttery dough beckoned me like a siren's call.

"Don't even think about it, Ben," Jacob warned, casting me a stern look as he set the plate down on the counter. "I'm putting these up high where you can't reach them."

A low whine escaped my throat, but I knew it was no use arguing as he gave me a final glance before leaving the kitchen to 'plug himself back in,' as the mistress often said.

Little did Jacob know the powers he was dealing with in a determined canine ... and my new devious feline accomplice!

The moment Jacob's back was turned, that kitty diva, Ember, slunk into the kitchen and sized up the situation. Spotting her opening, she leapt up onto the counter with effortless grace and began batting at the plate of iced buns playfully.

I watched in hopeless longing as she sampled the goods first, delicately lapping away the sugary glaze with her rough tongue. Once the icing was cleared, she used her claws to carve out succulent bites from the tender dough beneath.

That's when I made my move, bracing my front paws on the counter's edge so I could inhale those baked delicacies with big, ravenous gulps. They were every bit as heavenly as I'd imagined—light and fluffy with just the right amount of buttery richness.

Within moments, the dainty plate was licked clean, not a stray crumb or lingering sheen of icing to be found. I smacked my sugar-glazed chops with unabashed satisfaction as Ember busied herself with a contented grooming session.

Hours later, the sound of the front door opening signalled the master and mistress's return home from work. The delicious smells of dinner soon filled the air as the master bustled about the kitchen, preparing the evening meal. The family gathered around the table, enjoying their food and chatting about their day.

As the main course came to an end, Jacob perked up. "Oh! I almost forgot. I made iced finger buns in class today. They'll be perfect for dessert!"

He bounded into the kitchen, eager to retrieve his prized creations. But after a moment, his voice called out, sounding confused. "Dad? Where did you put the iced buns when you were cooking? I left them on the counter."

The master's brow furrowed. "Iced buns? I didn't see any iced buns when I was cooking, son."

Jacob reappeared in the doorway, his face a mask of disbelief. "What? But . . . I made them in class and brought them home. I put them right here on the counter!"

The family exchanged puzzled glances. "Are you sure you didn't leave them where Ben could get to them?" the mistress asked gently.

"Yes," Jacob insisted, his voice rising with frustration. "I remember putting them well out of his reach!"

Suddenly, Jacob's eyes narrowed as he glared at his siblings. "Adam, Bronwyn, did you guys eat them?"

Adam looked up from his phone, bewildered. "What? No way, I didn't even know you made iced buns."

Bronwyn shook her head vigorously. "Don't look at me."

"Well, someone must have eaten them!" Jacob exclaimed, his frustration mounting. "They didn't just disappear into thin air!"

At the mention of the missing treats, all eyes briefly turned to where I lounged on the living room floor. I fought to keep my expression neutral, far too stuffed to even bother begging pitifully.

Ember, perched regally on the sofa, simply licked her paw with languid disinterest, the picture of feline innocence.

"Well, I sure didn't eat them," the master chuckled.

As the family continued to speculate and Jacob grew increasingly exasperated, I couldn't help feeling a pang of guilt mixed with lingering satisfaction.

"Ugh, forget it!" Jacob finally threw up his hands in resignation. "I give up trying to enjoy any baked goods I make in this house. From now on, anything I bring home from that class goes straight into the fridge until it's time to eat it!"

My heart sank ever so slightly at those words. The refrigerator—that shining, air-tight vault against all my snacking aspirations. A worthy adversary, to be sure.

As Jacob stormed off muttering under his breath, with Adam and Bronwyn protesting their innocence behind him, I couldn't resist exchanging one last conspiratorial look with Ember. The battle over baked goods had only just begun for our unstoppable team!

Suki's Final Purr

Suki, our beloved feline companion, had been a constant presence in our home for as long as I could remember. Her gentle purrs and affectionate nuzzles had brought comfort and joy to the family for years. However, as time passed, it became evident that Suki's health was deteriorating.

At first, it was subtle changes—a slight loss of appetite, a decrease in her usually playful behaviour. The mistress, always attentive to the needs of her furry friends, noticed these changes and grew concerned. She began to monitor Suki's eating habits more closely, trying to entice her with her favourite treats and meals.

Despite her efforts, Suki continued to lose weight, her once plump frame becoming alarmingly thin. The family's worry grew as they watched their beloved cat struggle to maintain her usual routines. It wasn't long before another distressing symptom emerged: Suki had become incontinent, unable to control her bodily functions.

The mistress, her heart heavy with concern, made an appointment with the vet. I watched as she gently placed Suki in her carrier, whispering words of comfort and reassurance. The entire family waited anxiously for news, hoping against hope that there would be a solution, a way to help Suki regain her health.

When the mistress and master returned from the vet, their faces were sombre. The vet had confirmed that Suki's condition was terminal, and that there was nothing more that could be done. The kindest thing, the vet had said, would be to let Suki go, to end her suffering and allow her to pass peacefully.

The mistress, her voice choked with emotion, gently explained that prolonging Suki's life would only cause her more pain and discomfort.

I watched as the family gathered around Suki, showering her with love and affection in her final days. They took turns holding her, stroking her soft fur and whispering words of love and gratitude. Suki, despite her weakened state, seemed to sense the outpouring of love, her purrs growing softer and more content.

Suki's sister, May, who had been her constant companion and fellow mischief-maker, seemed to sense the change in the atmosphere. She would often curl up beside Suki, offering her warmth and comfort in her final days. It was as if May knew that their time together was coming to an end, and she wanted to make the most of every moment.

The day of the appointment arrived, and a heavy silence fell over the house. The mistress, her heart heavy with the weight of the impending loss, found herself unable to bring herself to take Suki to the vet. The thought of being present for Suki's final moments, knowing what was to come, was too much for her to bear.

The master, understanding the mistress's pain, stepped in to take on the difficult task. With a heavy heart, he gently lifted Suki into her carrier, his hands trembling slightly. The family gathered around, each taking a moment to say their final goodbyes. I, too, approached the carrier, my nose touching Suki's paw in a gesture of comfort and farewell. May watched from a distance, her eyes wide and questioning, as if she knew that Suki would not be returning.

As the master left with Suki, the mistress collapsed into tears, her body shaking with grief. The family gathered around her, offering words of comfort and support, knowing that the decision had been an incredibly difficult one for both the mistress and the master.

When the master returned, his face was drawn. He had found the experience of being with Suki in her final moments to be emotionally taxing, but he knew that it was a burden he had to bear for the sake of his beloved companion and his family.

In the days that followed, the house felt emptier, the absence of Suki's presence keenly felt. Her favourite spots remained untouched, as if waiting for her to return. May would often sit in these spots, as if seeking the familiar scent and comfort of her sister. She seemed lost without her companion, her usual playfulness diminished.

The family made sure to give May extra love and attention, knowing that she, too, was grieving the loss of her sister.

As time passed, the sharp edges of grief began to soften, replaced by a bittersweet acceptance. The family found solace in the knowledge that they had given Suki a life filled with love and happiness, and that her memory would forever be cherished in their hearts. May, too, began to heal, finding new joys and adventures, even as she carried the memory of her beloved sister with her.

Through the pain of Suki's loss, I witnessed the incredible strength and resilience of my human family. They had made the difficult decision to let Suki go, putting her needs before their own desires. It was a testament to the depth of their love and compassion, a reminder that sometimes the greatest act of love is letting go.

Binx

I was snoozing peacefully in a patch of warm sunlight when I heard the unmistakable sound of the front door opening. My ears perked up instantly. Any self-respecting watchdog knows that strange arrivals must be thoroughly inspected.

I trotted over to the entryway and was surprised to see Adam cradling a tiny bundle of fuzzy blackness in his arms. A new smell—unfamiliar, but not unpleasant—hit my nostrils. This must be investigated further.

I moved in closer, giving a cautious sniff. The small creature squirmed and I was shocked when two bright green eyes popped open to meet mine.

"Ben, this is our new kitten!" Adam said, kneeling so I could get a better look. "The last one of the litter. Isn't she just precious?"

She? I leaned in again, snout twitching. I wasn't so sure about that. There was something rather . . . masculine about this little fur ball.

The kitten stared at me, unblinking. We regarded each other for a moment before it let out a brazen "Mew!" as if to say, "Yeah, that's right, I'm here now. What of it?"

Well then! This feisty little thing was going to be a handful, I could already tell. But I couldn't help giving a doggy grin.

With those big innocent eyes and that quiet confidence, this kitten had me already wrapped around its paw.

Over the next few days, the kitten was doted on and cooed over relentlessly. A bright pink cat bed and matching dishes were purchased, as everyone was still operating under the misguided assumption that this kitten was female. I knew better, but I decided to keep that insight to myself for the moment.

It was quite amusing to watch the kitten assert its masculinity in little ways—sitting up proud and tall when it drank from that ridiculously frilly pink bowl, or batting around a crocheted pink ball without an ounce of self-consciousness. This little guy had style, I'd give him that.

Then one day, it finally became undeniable. The kitten was snuggled up in Mom's lap when she gasped, "Oh my! Well, don't those . . . appendages . . . make things clear!" She immediately started calling the kitten "him" and poor Adam had to make another trip to the pet store for a smart new blue collar.

From then on, the newly named Binx was part of the family. And I've got to admit, I was damn fond of that scruffy little rapscallion right from the start. We became inseparable partners in mischief, turning the garden into our playground and getting into side-splitting shenanigans daily.

Binx loved to chase me. I'd let him tackle me, and we'd giggle and wrestle in the grass like rambunctious pups. When I was tuckered out, he'd plop himself on my back and groom my ears with his scratchy little tongue. Eventually we'd settle down together, me on my side and Binx cuddled up against my belly, soaking up the warmth.

That silly cat could get under my skin like nobody's business. But I wouldn't have traded his company for anything in the world. Binx kept me feeling young and wonderfully annoyed in the best possible way. With him around, life just seemed fuller, richer, and twice as fun.

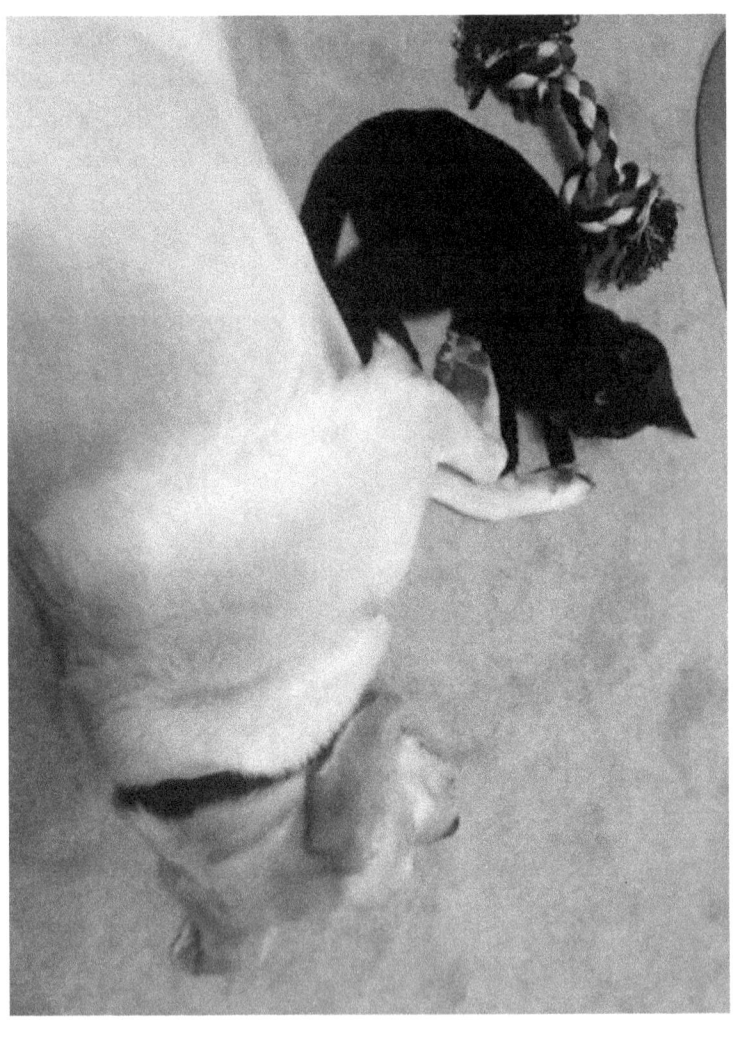

The Serenading Puss

With each passing season, that furry little terror Binx seemed to get bigger, bolder, and more audacious. What had started as an adorable kitten quickly morphed into a sleek, devilishly handsome cat with a taste for mischief. His confidence grew right alongside those piercing amber eyes and sharp little fangs.

While he had once been content to spend his days lounging in sunbeams and cuddling up to me for naps, Binx got antsy. He started meowing demandingly at the back door, wanting to be let out to explore the great outdoors on his own terms. Adam resisted at first, worried Binx would wander off and get lost or hurt. But that cat wouldn't be denied.

"Mrrrroooowww! Mrrrroowww!"

"Oh alright, you persistent fleabag. But you'd better come back, you hear me?" Adam would give in, cracking the door open. Binx would shoot out like a furry black bullet, sidling along the fence and ducking under bushes, already up to Lord-knows-what kinds of trouble.

At first, Adam would wait up long into the night for Binx's return. But that cat didn't seem to have any concept of a curfew. When he did finally slink back, Binx would make a beeline for Adam's bedroom, scratching impatiently at the window.

"Mrrrrow? Mrrrrooooowwww!"

The whole family would be jolted awake by that insistent, raspy yowl in the darkness.

"Ugh, alright, alright! Hold your horses!" Adam would grumble, stumbling out of bed to let the furry desperado inside.

Binx would spin dramatically around Adam's ankles, tail arched over his back, revelling in his own glorious homecoming. Then he'd make a big show of grooming himself, daring anyone to ask where he'd been or what he'd been up to. When he was finally satisfied with his appearance, Binx would saunter over to the bed and settle in against Adam's side with a possessive purr, as if to say, "That's right, peasants. I'm back. All is right in the kingdom once more."

This ridiculous routine played out night after night. The rest of us—humans and dog alike—were left as bleary-eyed observers, mere subjects in Binx's royal court.

Then things got out of hand when Adam moved out to live with his girlfriend Becky. Adam knew that Binx was settled and a permanent member of my pack and so asked the mistress if she would continue taking care of him. With Adam's departure came the opportunity to change the bedrooms around and Binx's nocturnal wakings became his younger sister Bronwyn's problem.

"Mrrrooowww! Mrrroooooowwwww!"

"Oh come on, Binx, it's 3 am! Give it a rest already!" Bronwyn would yell, burying her head under the pillow and cursing that cat's extended nighttime escapades.

But Binx was relentless. He'd scratch and yowl at her window until it opened, then make a beeline for the bed and Bronwyn's feet. If she shooed him away, he'd just slink back over and make himself comfortable on top of the covers.

You had to admire his sheer dogged determination, I'll give the furball that. Bronwyn grew so exhausted and sleep-deprived from Binx's window serenades that she finally balked.

"That's it! I can't take this anymore," she declared one morning, dark circles ringing her eyes. "I'm trading bedrooms with Mom and Dad. This diva cat can be their problem."

All change again! The mistress and master got stuck on permanent cat-sitting duty once more, all because of a certain spoiled furry prince's unshakeable habits.

I tried to be a good friend and give Binx a gentle lecture about respecting people's sleep schedules, but he just blinked slowly and licked his chops, as if to say, "Sorry old pal, a cat's gotta do what a cat's gotta do. No regrets, baby!"

That rascally cat lived by his own code, rules be damned. I couldn't help snorting out a grudgingly admiring chortle. Infuriating as he could be, you had to respect the guy's brazen sense of feline privilege.

Binx did whatever he wanted, whenever he wanted—and Lord help any mere human who tried to get in his way!

The Black Dog

It was a gradual thing, the way the darkness crept into our lives. At first, it was just a shadow, a flicker at the edge of my vision. But as time went on, it grew bolder, more substantial. It took on a shape, a form. And before I knew it, it had a name.

The Black Dog.

That's what the mistress called it, this thing that haunted her. She'd always been such a vibrant soul, full of energy and life. She was the one who took me on long rambles through the fields, who threw the ball for me until her arm ached, who always had a kind word and a cuddle no matter how tired she was.

But then, something changed. It was like the light inside her dimmed, fading away bit by bit. She moved more slowly, wincing with every step. She'd spend hours on the couch, staring into space, her eyes dull and distant.

At first, I thought she was just under the weather. We all have our off days, after all. But as the weeks stretched into months, I realised this was something more. Something bigger, and darker, and more insidious.

The master took her to the vet—the human vet, that is. The doctor. They ran tests, poked and prodded, asked endless questions. And finally, they gave it a name.

Fibromyalgia. Myalgic Encephalomyelitis. ME/CFS.

I didn't understand the words, but I could see the toll they took on my mistress. Fibromyalgia, the mistress had explained to my pack, was a condition that caused widespread pain, fatigue, and tenderness in the muscles and joints. ME/CFS, short for Myalgic Encephalomyelitis/Chronic Fatigue Syndrome, was similar, characterised by profound exhaustion, cognitive difficulties, and a host of other symptoms.

Together, they were a one-two punch that left my mistress reeling. She'd always been so active, so full of vigour. Now, just getting out of bed in the morning was a Herculean task. She'd force herself through the day, putting on a brave face, but I could see the pain etched in the lines around her eyes, the weariness that clung to her like a second skin.

And then, there was the Black Dog.

It wasn't a real dog, of course. Not like me. It was more of a metaphor, a way of describing the depression that so often accompanies chronic illness. But to me, it might as well have been a tangible thing. I could sense its presence, lurking in the shadows, waiting to pounce.

On bad days, when the pain was at its worst and the fatigue was overwhelming, the Black Dog would make itself known. It would curl up next to the mistress, a heavy weight on her chest, whispering dark thoughts into her ear. I could see it in the slump of her shoulders, the emptiness in her gaze.

Those were the days I stuck closest to her side. I'd lay my head on her lap, nuzzling her hand until she stroked my ears. I'd bring her my favourite toys, hoping to coax a smile. I'd stay near her, a constant presence, a reminder that she wasn't alone.

You see, we dogs have a sixth sense about these things. We can pick up on the subtlest changes in our human's moods, their behaviour, even their scent. When something's wrong, we just know.

In the case of the mistress, I could smell the sickness on her, a sour tang that clung to her skin. I could hear the hitch in her breathing when the pain was bad, the soft groans she tried to hide. I could feel the tremors in her hands as she stroked my fur, the way her muscles would tense and spasm under my weight.

And I could sense the despair, the hopelessness that threatened to consume her. It was like a black hole, a yawning void that sucked the joy out of everything. It scared me, seeing her like that. I was just a dog, after all. What could I do in the face of such darkness?

But I did what I could. I was there for her, a constant companion, a warm body to lean on. When she'd cry, I'd lick the tears from her cheeks. When she couldn't sleep, I'd curl up beside her, my steady breathing a lullaby. When the pain made her snap, I'd forgive her, knowing it wasn't really me she was angry at.

And you know what? It helped. Oh, it didn't cure her, of course. I'm not some magical panacea. But having me there, a faithful friend, a nonjudgmental listener . . . it made a difference.

That's the thing about us dogs. We have a way of getting under your skin, into your heart. We love unconditionally, wholly, and completely. We don't care if you're sick or sad or cranky. We just want to be near you, to comfort you, to make you feel less alone.

It's a powerful thing, that kind of love. It has a way of chasing away the shadows, of making even the darkest days a little bit brighter. And for the mistress, in her battle with the Black Dog, it was a lifeline.

There were still bad days, of course. Days when she couldn't get out of bed, when the pain was so bad she'd weep into my fur. Days when the Black Dog's hold seemed unbreakable, when hope was a distant memory.

But there were good days, too. Days when she'd manage a short walk around the block, leaning on me for support. Days when she'd laugh at my antics, her eyes sparkling with something close to their old light. Days when the future didn't seem quite so bleak, quite so hopeless.

And through it all, I was there. Her constant companion, her stalwart friend. The one being in the world who loved her unconditionally, who saw past the illness and the pain to the beautiful soul beneath.

It wasn't always easy. There were times I felt helpless, times I wished I could do more. But I did what I could, in my own small way. I was her comfort, her solace, her reason to keep going even when the Black Dog was nipping at her heels.

And you know what? I wouldn't have traded it for anything. Because that's what love is, in the end. It's being there, through the good times and the bad. It's seeing someone at their worst and loving them anyway. It's facing the darkness together, side by side, paw in hand.

The mistress's battle with fibromyalgia, with ME/CFS, with the Black Dog...it was ongoing. There were no easy answers, no quick fixes. But she wasn't fighting alone. She had me, and the master, and a whole network of friends and family who loved her.

And bit by bit, day by day, we pushed back against the darkness. We celebrated the small victories, the little moments of joy and laughter amidst the pain. We clung to hope, even when it seemed fragile as a butterfly's wing.

I won't lie and say it was a fairy tale ending. Chronic illness doesn't work that way. There were still days when the Black Dog's shadow loomed large. There were still nights when the mistress cried herself to sleep, her body wracked with pain.

But there were also moments of grace, of beauty, of love so fierce it took my breath away. Moments when I'd catch the mistress looking at me, her eyes soft and brimming with gratitude. Moments when she'd bury her face in my fur and whisper, "I don't know what I'd do without you, Benny Boo."

And in those moments, I knew I was exactly where I was meant to be. Not just a dog, but a healer, a guardian, a light in the darkness. The mistress's champion, her protector, her friend.

Together, we faced the Black Dog. Together, we walked through the shadows. And together, we found our way back to the light.

It wasn't always easy, and it wasn't always pretty. But it was real, and it was true, and it was ours. A bond forged in the fire of adversity, tempered by the power of unconditional love.

And in the end, that was enough. More than enough. It was everything.

So to all the Black Dogs out there, to all the shadows that threaten to overwhelm . . . I say this. You may be big, and you may be scary. But you've never met the likes of me and my mistress.

We're a team, she, and I. A force to be reckoned with. And together . . . together, we can face anything.

Even you.

The Walk

One of the greatest joys in a dog's life is 'The Walk.' There's just nothing quite like getting out into the great outdoors, putting that nose to the ground, and seeing what new sniffs and adventures the day will bring. My favourite part was always the few blessed moments at the start when I'd be unleashed and could go romping freely through the fields.

Imagine my delight when that rapscallion Binx decided he wanted in on the action after the mistress fell ill and the master took over walking duties. It started with Binx just tagging along, trotting a few paces behind me and the master. But then the little furball got bolder, venturing ahead to lead the way.

"Where do you think you're going, you mangy fur ball?" I'd growl, letting my voice get all grumbly and exaggerated like I was some terrifying junkyard dog. Binx would just flick his tail sassily and keep on strutting.

"You trying to take over my walk? This is my 'hood, cat!"

Binx would stop, turn around with those big innocent eyes, and coolly lick a paw as if to say, "What, this old thing? You don't mind if I tag along, do you?"

Cheeky little fuzzball.

When the master would finally unfasten my leash with a "Be good, boys!" Binx and I would both take off at full tilt down the path. I'd race ahead on my longer legs, but Binx was freakishly quick for someone so small. We'd streak through the tall grass, leaping over logs, dodging trees, not a care in the world.

Eventually I'd let Binx think he'd gotten ahead of me. But then I'd double back through the bushes and leap out at him from behind, growling playfully. He'd puff out his fur and take a swiping stance, ready to defend his honour like a tiny wilderness wildcat. I'd lick him right in the face and he'd crumple into an undignified giggling mass of fur as I smothered him in slobbery doggy kisses.

"Ben! Binx! You two! Get over here right now before I put you both on lockdown," the master would call in that voice that meant he wasn't kidding around. We'd catch our breath, share a conspiratorial grin, and lollop back over to rejoin our human.

"Heel, Ben. And you, Binx—don't even think about it!" he'd bark out in that tone I knew meant we were toeing the line.

Binx would stop in his tracks, all big eyes and innocence. But I could see the mischievous gears turning behind those amber peepers. As soon as the master's back was turned, here came that sly kitty darting off into the bushes again with a flick of his tail, silently daring me to give chase.

How could I resist? With an apologetic glance at the master's stern expression, I'd go bounding off after Binx, crashing through the underbrush and barking up a storm. The furry little instigator would stay tantalisingly ahead of me, leading me on a merry cat-and-mouse chase until finally I'd skid to a halt, panting heavily.

"You . . . are . . . incorrigible!" I'd huff out between lapping breaths of air. Binx's whiskers would twitch as if he were suppressing a laugh.

The master's voice would carry through the trees then. "Ben, where are you? You come back here this instant, you hear?"

Tail and ears drooping, I'd slink back through the bushes to rejoin the master, Binx slinking sassily along behind me. The master would fix us both with a disappointed glare.

"Do I need to get the both of you leashes? Because I will, so help me," he'd grumble, jabbing a finger at Binx who simply blinked insolently. "This nonsense stops now, you hear me?"

We'd both hang our heads, chastised. But as soon as the master's back was turned again, leading us back home, Binx would shoot me a sideways look. His eyes danced with unrepentant mirth, telling me plain as day:

"Same time tomorrow, eh pup?"

Walk on the Wild Side

Trotting down the road with Binx by my side, I was in doggy heaven. There's nothing quite like a morning constitutional to get the blood pumping and the tail wagging, especially with my best feline friend along for the ride.

As we rounded the corner, I caught a whiff of something intriguing on the breeze. Was that bacon I detected? My nose twitched in anticipation, but before I could investigate further, I heard squealing brakes.

I looked up to see the postman gawking at us through his van window, mouth hanging open in disbelief. He pulled to a stop at the end of the road, then slowly reversed until he was alongside us again.

Binx and I paused, tilting our heads quizzically at the interruption to our walk. The postman leaned out of his window, blinking rapidly as if trying to clear his vision.

"Well I'll be," he muttered, shaking his head. "A dog and a cat, walking together bold as brass. And not a growl or a hiss between 'em. Amazing..."

I sat down, giving the man my friendliest grin. I knew we must look a bit odd—a strapping young Labrador and a sleek black cat, out for a stroll like a pair of old chums.

Binx, meanwhile, fixed the postman with a withering stare, as if to say, "Yes, and? Can't a cat enjoy a constitutional with his canine comrade without causing a public scene?"

The postman let out an incredulous chuckle. "What a sight you two are," he said, grinning from ear to ear. "The most unlikely of pals. Well, you've made my day, you have."

With a final shake of his head, he put his van in gear and drove off, no doubt eager to regale his mates back at the depot with tales of the extraordinary thing he'd witnessed on his morning rounds.

I glanced at Binx. Binx glanced at me. If cats could shrug, I swear he would have. His expression seemed to say, "Humans. So easily impressed by the mundane."

I let out a little "Woof" of agreement. Honestly, was it so strange? A dog and a cat, putting aside their differences and enjoying each other's company? Maybe to some narrow-minded types, but to us, it just felt ... natural.

We continued on our way, paws falling into that easy synchronicity we'd perfected over our many walks together. The scents of the morning filled my nose - damp earth, fresh cut grass, the tantalising aroma of frying bacon wafting from a nearby kitchen.

Up ahead, I spotted a squirrel darting along a low garden wall. I felt my muscles tense, ready to spring into pursuit. But then I caught Binx's eye and remembered our pact—no chasing, no shenanigans, just two civilized gents out for a morning stroll.

Binx gave me a little nod of approval, as if to say, "Attaboy, Ben. Knew you could resist temptation."

And you know what? That felt just as satisfying as sinking my teeth into any bushy-tailed rodent. Because here I was, Benjamin the Labrador, out for a walk with my main man Binx. Two amigos. Compadres in arms. The most unlikely of BFFs, but friends all the same.

As we turned the corner towards home, I couldn't help but wag my tail in contentment. Let the postman stare. Let the world marvel at our unconventional bond. This was us—Ben and Binx, marching to the beat of our own drum, one paw in front of the other.

And I wouldn't have had it any other way.

Field of Dreams (and Feathers)

It was a day like any other—or so I thought—as the master clipped on my leash for our usual romp in the park fields. Little did I know, adventure was about to come calling in a big way.

As we set off down the drive, I could feel a certain spring in my step. The sun was shining, the birds were singing, and the wide open expanse of the field beckoned invitingly. Even Binx seemed more chipper than usual, his tail held high as he trotted along beside me.

We'd just reached the far end of the field when it happened. A fat, juicy pigeon waddled out from the tall grass right in front of us, practically begging to be chased. I felt a surge of primal doggy instinct take over. Before I knew what was happening, I lunged forward with all my might.

SNAP! The leash broke clean away from my collar, and I was off like a shot, paws pounding the earth as I hurtled after that ball of feathers.

"Ben! BEN! Get back here!" I heard the master shout behind me, but I was too far gone to pay any heed. The thrill of the chase consumed me entirely.

I tore across the field, sending birds of all descriptions scattering in a flurry of wings and alarmed chirps. The pigeon fluttered madly ahead of me, just out of reach. I put on an extra burst of speed, determined to catch my quarry.

Suddenly, a black streak shot past me in a blur of fur. Binx! That wily cat had joined the pursuit, and he was gaining on the pigeon fast. His lithe feline body was built for speed and agility in a way my bulky Labrador frame just wasn't.

"It's mine!" I barked, redoubling my efforts. "I saw it first!"

Binx flicked an ear back at me as if to say, "You snooze, you lose, pup!"

We whipped around a clump of bushes and charged across a patch of wildflowers. I could hear the distant shouts of the master as he tried to catch up to us, but we were too focused on our avian prize to care.

Just as Binx was about to make his move, the pigeon veered sharply to the right. Quick as a flash, Binx changed direction . . . and promptly lost his footing on a hidden hole. He tumbled head over tail, landing in an undignified heap.

I saw my chance and seized it. Putting on one last mighty burst of speed, I closed the gap and pounced. I felt the satisfying squish of feathers in my mouth as my jaws closed around the bird. Victory was mine!

But my elation was short-lived. No sooner had I clamped down on my prize than I felt a pair of hands grab me firmly by the scruff.

"Got you, you little scamp!" the master panted, his face red from exertion. "What do you think you're playing at, taking off like that? You nearly gave me a heart attack!"

I dropped the stunned pigeon, which fluttered dazedly off into the safety of the trees, and turned to give the master my best "sorry, not sorry" grin. Binx limped over, looking rather worse for wear, with twigs and leaves stuck in his usually immaculate coat.

The master fixed us both with a stern glare. "Don't think I didn't see you egging him on," he said to Binx, who had the grace to look mildly sheepish. "You're both in big trouble, you hear? No treats for a week!"

I hung my head, trying to look appropriately contrite. But inside, I was still buzzing with the thrill of the chase. From the gleam in Binx's eye, I could tell he felt the same. Sure, we might be in the doghouse (or cat condo) for a while, but it had been worth it for those few glorious moments of unbridled freedom.

As the master clipped a spare leash to my collar and led us out of the field, I couldn't resist shooting Binx a conspiratorial wink. He replied with a sly flick of his tail, a silent promise passing between us.

We'd be back to chase another day, come what may. After all, what's an adventure without a little mischief?

Dental Despair

Something seemed . . . off . . . with May. The usually affectionate tabby had become a ghost, slinking through the house like she didn't want to be seen. She started avoiding all of us—even Jacob, her favourite human who she typically showered with cuddles and headbutts. Instead of curling up in a sunny patch to welcome pets and scratches, May took to hunkering under the kitchen table, back arched and a low growl rumbling in her throat whenever someone passed too close.

"What's gotten into that crazy cat?" the master wondered aloud when May remained stubbornly hidden during her usual treat time. He reached a hand under the table to coax her out, giving a sharp yelp when her paw shot out to swipe at him. "Yowch! Well then!"

I cautiously stuck my nose under the table to see what the fuss was about. May's green eyes were wide and wild, her tabby stripes stark against the shadows. An acrid, sour smell hung thick in the air—a tell-tale sign that something wasn't right health wise.

"Mrrrrowww!" she hissed, swiping a paw to emphasise her demand to be left alone. I pulled my head back out quickly before those claws could connect.

"Easy there, girl. No need to get snippy," I mumbled, shooting a concerned look toward the mistress. May had always been the most sociable of the femme feline crew—purring, playful, cuddling up with my pack in turn like an affectionate little furry heat pack. To see her so withdrawn and aggressive set off alarms in my doggy brain.

Over the next few days, May's behaviour grew even more erratic and reclusive. We could hear her pacing restlessly through the house at night, howling out plaintive, miserable yowls that set my fur on end. When the mistress tried to corner her to get a look at what might be bothering her, May just flattened her ears and bolted away, disappearing into another hiding spot.

"That's it, we're taking her to the vet," the master declared after May started turning her nose up at her food bowls too. "Something is seriously wrong here."

Catching her proved easier said than done though. May put up such a ferocious struggle, hissing and batting at the pet carrier once she was finally trapped inside, that the mistress emerged with bloody scratches scoring both arms.

I watched anxiously as they loaded May into the car and drove away. The house felt eerily quiet without her presence, and I paced restlessly, waiting for their return.

Hours passed, and when the master and mistress finally came home, their faces were drawn and their eyes red-rimmed. My heart sank as I realized May wasn't with them.

From the snippets of conversation I overheard, I pieced together what had happened. The vet had discovered an abscessed tooth that had led to a dangerous infection called sepsis. Despite their best efforts and immediate treatment with IV antibiotics, the infection had spread too quickly.

"I can't believe she's gone," the mistress sobbed into the master's shoulder. "If only we'd noticed sooner..."

Jacob was inconsolable, locking himself in his room and refusing to come out. The whole house seemed to be shrouded in a heavy blanket of grief.

That night, we sat in numb silence around the fireplace, feeling the gaping loss of May's bright, loving presence. How could this little tabby we all adored so much be gone, just like that? The vet's warnings about feline dental disease and how rapidly an infection can turn deadly kept echoing through the house.

From then on, the mistress and master were fastidious about our dental care: daily tooth brushings with special animal-safe toothpaste, dental chews and greenies for snacks, and a foul-tasting powder supplement that was dusted over every meal to fight plaque and bacteria.

None of us furred folk enjoyed that vile powder staining our food bowls. The remaining cats in particular staged full-blown hunger strikes, refusing to come near their tainted meals and meowing pitifully while shooting dagger eyes at the mistress.

But she was unmoved, simply scooping up the refused food and stashing it in the fridge once the designated mealtime had passed.

"You'll eat it sooner or later, Your Majesties," she'd say with a quirked brow in the cats' direction. "Unless you'd like to starve?"

We'd all shuffle our paws, but the cats quickly caved first each time. Feline superiority only stretched so far when an empty belly started growling. One by one, those uppity fur balls would slink over to their dishes, countering each hesitant lick with a disdainful sniff as if to say, "The indignities I suffer for you peasants!"

I'd just chow down happily, giving appreciative licks to the bowl when I'd cleaned it. Hey, the powder was gross but it beat the alternative—ending up like poor May. If crunching some unsavoury grub was all it took to stay healthy and happy by my humans' sides for as long as possible, I'd stomach it without a second thought. because a pawful of bad-tasting supplements was a small price to pay for getting to keep living my best doggy life, surrounded by my beloved (if sometimes unreasonable) crew of humans and remaining cats. I'd do anything to avoid another devastating loss like when we had to say goodbye to our sweet little tabby May.

Brushed teeth, bodged-up bowls, regular check-ups—whatever it took to stick around, I was game. After witnessing how quickly an untreated infection could turn catastrophic, none of us took any chances with our dental hygiene again. We were in this furry life together, come what may—the good, the bad and yes, even the occasional disgusting powder-laced meal.

Nana Lynda and the Endless Belly Rubs

I heard the familiar sound of the doorbell and the clacking of Nana Lynda's shoes on the hardwood floor as my mistress let her in. My tail started wagging instinctively - Nana Lynda's visits always meant lots of head scratches, belly rubs and, of course, extra treats.

When Nana Lynda used to live with us, I could tell she wasn't quite sure what to make of me at first. A big, bouncing golden lab had probably looked more like a slobbery beast than a cuddly companion in her eyes. But being the master of charm that I am, it hadn't taken long for me to win her over.

I trotted over to greet Nana Lynda as she came in. "Well hello there, Ben!" she cooed, bending down to ruffle the fur on my head. "Aren't you just the most handsome dog?!" Her hands were so soft and her voice so cheerful, I couldn't help but lean into her, pressing my bulk against her legs.

"Oof, careful Ben!" Nana Lynda chuckled as she wobbled a bit. "You're not exactly a small dog, you know."

I gazed up at her innocently. I knew my puppy-dog eyes were irresistible, even if I wasn't a puppy anymore. "Oh alright, you big lug, let's go sit down so I can give you a proper cuddle."

As we made our way to the living room, I noticed the cat, Ember, already circling around Nana Lynda's feet. She was usually aloof, but something about Nana Lynda turned her into a purring, rubbing, attention-seeking feline.

I watched as Nana Lynda settled herself on the couch, placing her coat and handbag beside her. Almost immediately, Ember jumped up and started rubbing herself against her coat, her tail sticking straight up in the air.

"What is it with you and that coat, Ember?" my mistress laughed, coming in with tea and biscuits. "It's like it's made of catnip or something."

Nana Lynda chuckled, giving Ember a scratch under the chin. "Maybe it's my perfume. I do wear one that has a bit of a floral scent. Maybe they like that."

Ember started to rub herself against Nana's handbag, purring loudly and completely lost in her own kitty euphoria. I felt a slight pang of jealousy. I mean, I knew I was Nana Lynda's favourite, but did the cat have to make it so obvious that she adored her too?

Deciding it was time to reclaim my rightful place as the centre of Nana Lynda's attention, I practically pranced over to her, eager for the belly rub session I knew was coming. Nana Lynda patted her knees invitingly. I flopped down on her feet, not so gracefully.

She laughed and shook her head. I just panted happily in response as she began stroking my tummy, her fingers gently massaging that sweet spot that made my back leg start kicking involuntarily.

"He sure loves his Nana Lynda, doesn't he?" my mistress remarked with a smile.

I caught a whiff of the ginger biscuits and perked up, drool already starting to pool under my tongue. Labradors like me are notorious for our love of all things edible. Our powerful noses can sniff out food from impressive distances and our stomachs seem to have no limit. But all that enthusiastic eating can pack on the pounds quickly if we're not careful.

I put on my most winsome expression, eyes round and pleading as I looked from the biscuits to Nana Lynda meaningfully.

"Now Ben, don't start begging," my mistress warned. But Nana was already reaching for a biscuit.

"Oh let him have one, the poor dear looks so hopeful," she said, holding the treat out to me. I took it from her hand, my tail sweeping back and forth.

"You're spoiling him, Lynda," my mistress sighed. "Remember, he's meant to be on a diet. The vet said he needs to watch his weight to stay healthy. Labradors are prone to obesity, you know."

This was true. We labs may be strong, athletic dogs, but excess weight gain can lead to all sorts of health problems down the road, like joint pain, diabetes, even shortened lifespans. I knew my mistress was just looking out for me, even if my stomach protested the strict portion control.

"A little treat now and then won't hurt," Nana Lynda said conspiratorially, breaking off another bit of biscuit and slipping it to me. I gobbled it up, licking her fingers appreciatively. My mistress just rolled her eyes good-naturedly. She knew when it came to me and Nana Lynda, resistance was futile.

As I settled back into Nana Lynda's ministrations, I rested my head on her lap, gazing up at her adoringly. "Oh Ben, is that a foot you feel under your paw?" she asked with mock seriousness. I shifted my bulk pointedly. "Well, I suppose there are worse things than being a footrest to such a handsome fella."

And so it became our thing—every time Nana Lynda visited from her new flat, I would plop myself on her feet, pinning her in place so the ear scratches and belly rubs could commence. Ember would circle and rub against her coat and handbag, drawn to her like a moth to a flame. And my mistress would look on, shaking her head at the hold Nana Lynda seemed to have over all of us furry creatures.

Sometimes my mistress would scold Nana Lynda for overindulging me, but I knew I had a devoted ally in Nana Lynda. With her, I could do no wrong. I was her "handsome boy", her "darling dog", and she was my soft-hearted treat dispenser and cuddle buddy extraordinaire.

"You know, Lynda," my mistress said one day as Nana Lynda slipped me yet another morsel under the table when she had stayed for tea. "I read that labradors are the most likely breed to be obese. Something about a gene mutation that makes them extra food-motivated."

"Is that so?" Nana Lynda replied, glancing down at me. I wagged my tail hopefully, eyeing the last bit of sausage in her hand. "Well, I suppose that explains a lot."

"Mmmhmm," my mistress nodded. "That's why it's so important to keep them active and not overfeed them, no matter how persuasive their begging might be." She gave Nana Lynda a pointed look.

Nana Lynda had the grace to look a bit sheepish. "I know, I know. I just can't resist this face." She cupped my muzzle affectionately. "But you're right, we need to keep this boy healthy. What do you say, Ben? Ready for a nice long walk to work off those treats?"

I leapt up, tail wagging furiously. A walk? With Nana Lynda? And then maybe more belly rubs after? It was like all my doggy dreams were coming true.

As we set off down the street, Nana Lynda keeping a firm grip on my leash as I strained ahead, eager to explore, I thought about how lucky I was. Sure, I knew I needed to keep my svelte figure, but I figured a little extra love and some stealthy snacks courtesy of my favourite Nana was worth having to trek a couple more laps around the park. With a grandmother like her, I was one lucky lab indeed, even if I wasn't a puppy anymore.

"Good boy, Ben," Nana Lynda praised as I trotted obediently at her side.

I glanced up at her, my chocolate brown eyes full of adoration. Nana Lynda really was the best. With her by my side and a whole park full of exciting smells ahead, I was pretty sure this old dog had plenty more happy times ahead—if there were plenty of belly rubs, biscuits, and maybe a few envious glances from the feline diva when she saw who Nana Lynda's real favourite was.

A Tail of Two Terriers

It was a beautiful day for a stroll, the kind of day that just begs you to get out and sniff the roses (or the lamp posts, as the case may be). The master had me on my extendable lead as Binx and I made our usual rounds, enjoying the sunshine and each other's company as we walked down the street towards the park.

We were just passing by a neighbour's house when it happened. Now, this neighbour is a lovely lady, always quick with a pat on the head and a "Who's a good boy then?" but she's not exactly what you'd call attentive when it comes to matters of home security.

Case in point: her garden gate. It was one of those old, rickety wooden affairs, held closed more by habit than by any actual lock. And today, as luck would have it, it stood slightly ajar, as if someone had forgotten to close it properly.

I caught a whiff of something on the air—a scent I didn't recognise. It was canine, but not like any dog I knew from the neighbourhood. There was a wildness to it, an unfamiliar edge that set my hackles rising.

Before I could even bark out a warning, a huge, shaggy shape came bounding out from behind the gate. It was a dog, alright— the biggest, meanest-looking dog I'd ever seen. And it was off leash, free to roam and terrorise as it pleased.

The beast skidded to a halt, its eyes locking onto Binx. I could see the predatory gleam in its gaze, the way its muscles tensed for the chase. Binx, to his credit, barely batted an eye. He just stared coolly back at the hulking canine, his tail swishing lazily.

"Well now," I heard him purr under his breath. "What have we here? A little lost lamb, so far from the flock?"

The dog let out a thunderous growl that seemed to shake the very pavement. "Cat," it snarled, licking its chops. "I love chasing cats. And this is my territory. You'd best run along home, kitty, before I decide to make a snack of you."

I felt my own growl building in my throat. Who did this mangy mutt think he was, threatening my best friend? I lunged forward, my extendable lead unspooling rapidly as I put myself between Binx and the bristling behemoth.

The master, startled by my sudden movement, fumbled with the lead. "Ben, heel!" he commanded, but I was too focused on the threat at hand to obey.

"Now see here, pal," I barked, my lead taut as a bowstring. "This here's a public path. And that there's my partner in crime you're talking to. So why don't you just shuffle on back to your garden and we'll say no more about it, hmm?"

The dog threw back its head and laughed, a harsh, barking sound that set my teeth on edge. "Oh, that's rich," it chuckled nastily. "A tubby little lapdog, playing the hero. Tell you what, Fido—I'll give you to the count of three to get out of my way. Then the cat's mine. One..."

I glanced back at Binx, hoping for some kind of plan. But the infuriating feline just yawned, looking bored by the whole proceedings. "Wake me when it's over, would you, Ben old chum?" he drawled. "I fancy a bit of a catnap."

"Two..." the dog growled, crouching low like a sprinter at the starting block.

I swallowed hard, my mind racing. What was I supposed to do now? I was tethered to the master, but he seemed frozen in shock, unable to intervene. It was up to me to protect Binx.

"Three!" the dog roared, and suddenly it was charging, a furry freight train of fangs and fury.

I braced myself, ready to meet the beast head-on. But at the last possible moment, that crafty cat leapt into action. With a grace that bordered on insulting, he sprang straight up into the air, using my back as a springboard to launch himself even higher.

The dog, caught off guard, tried to skid to a halt. But it had too much momentum built up. It went barrelling past me, its jaws snapping shut on empty air as Binx soared overhead.

I spun around, trying to keep the dog in my sights. But my lead, still held tight in the master's grip, limited my movement. I could only watch as the dog wheeled around, ready for another pass.

But Binx was ready for it. As the dog charged again, he darted nimbly to the side, sending the mutt careening into a nearby hedge. The dog yelped as it collided with the prickly branches, thrashing and flailing as it tried to untangle itself.

Binx, meanwhile, had scampered up the fence, peering down at the struggling dog with an expression of amused disdain.

"Tsk tsk," he tutted, shaking his head. "Such a temper. Didn't your mother ever teach you to look before you leap?"

The dog, finally freeing itself from the hedge, glared up at Binx with murder in its eyes. "You think you're so clever, don't you?" it growled, bits of twig and leaf stuck in its fur. "But you can't stay up there forever. And when you come down . . ."

"Oh, I wouldn't worry about that," Binx interrupted, examining his claws nonchalantly. "You see, unlike some creatures, I actually use my brain before engaging in foolish pursuits. Case in point . . ."

He nodded towards the front door, where a familiar figure was rapidly exiting. She did not look happy.

"Whiskey!" she shrieked, her face a mask of horror as she took in the scene. "What have you done? Bad dog! Bad, bad dog!"

The dog—Whiskey, apparently—immediately cowered, its tail tucking between its legs. It slunk over to its owner, head hanging low, the very picture of canine contrition.

"Oh, I'm so sorry!" she apologised as she clipped a lead to Whiskey's collar. "He's never done anything like this before! I don't know what got into him! I hope he didn't hurt anyone?"

"No harm done," the master assured her, though his voice shook slightly. I could tell he was rattled by the close call. "Just maybe keep a closer eye on him in the future, yeah?"

She nodded vigorously, already dragging Whiskey back inside their house. The dog shot one last baleful glare over its shoulder at Binx, who simply smirked in return.

As they disappeared, Binx hopped down from his perch, landing lightly beside me. "Well," he said, giving a luxurious stretch. "That was bracing, wasn't it? Nothing like a spot of morning exercise to work up an appetite."

I gaped at him, my adrenaline still pumping. "Bracing?" I repeated incredulously. "Binx, that monster nearly turned us both into mincemeat! How can you be so calm about it?"

Binx shrugged, his tail curling into a question mark. "What can I say?" he purred. "When you've got nine lives to spare, you learn not to sweat the small stuff. Besides," he added, butting his head against my shoulder affectionately, "I knew I had you to watch my back. My very own knight in shining collar."

I felt a swell of pride at his words, my chest puffing out involuntarily. "Well, of course," I said, trying to sound nonchalant. "That's what friends are for, right? Sticking together, no matter what."

"Quite right," Binx agreed, a rare note of sincerity in his voice. "And there's no one I'd rather have by my side than you, Ben old boy. Even if you do have a distressing tendency to leap before you look."

I chuckled, giving him a playful nudge. "Hey, that's part of my charm," I protested. "Life's no fun without a little risk now and then."

"If you say so," Binx sighed, but I could see the glint of amusement in his eyes. "Just try not to make a habit of it, hmm? I'm rather fond of you, you know. I'd hate to see you end up as some mangy mutt's chew toy."

"Aww, Binx," I grinned, my tail wagging furiously. "I didn't know you cared."

"Yes, well," Binx sniffed, looking suddenly very interested in a passing butterfly. "Don't let it go to your head. Come on, let's get moving before anything else exciting happens. I think we've had quite enough adventure for one day."

And with that, he set off down the street, his tail held high. I fell into step beside him, my lead once again slack as the master followed behind us.

As we walked, I couldn't help but marvel at the twists and turns the day had taken. From a peaceful morning stroll to a heart-stopping showdown, all in the space of a few minutes. But then, that was life with Binx—always unpredictable, never boring. And I wouldn't have traded it for all the biscuits in the world.

Friendship is all about sticking together through thick and thin, facing down whatever challenges come your way. Whether it's a rampaging rabbit or a rogue terrier, I knew that if I had Binx by my side, I could handle anything.

And that, my friends, is a bond worth more than all the buried bones in creation.

The Curious Case of the Coprophagic Canine

It was a habit that confounded and disgusted my humans in equal measure. A habit that, try as I might, I just couldn't seem to shake. A habit that had become the bane of their existence and the source of endless frustration for all involved.

I'm talking, of course, about my penchant for raiding the cat litter tray and helping myself to the delectable nuggets within.

Now, I know what you're thinking. "Ben, that's revolting! Why on earth would you want to eat cat poo?" And believe me, I've asked myself the same question many times. It's not like it's a particular gourmet experience. The texture is gritty, the flavour is...well, let's just say it's an acquired taste.

But here's the thing: to a dog, cat droppings are like a fine delicacy. It's a phenomenon known as coprophagia, and it's surprisingly common among canines. There are a few theories as to why we do it.

Some experts say it's a holdover from our wild ancestry. Back when dogs were more closely related to wolves, eating faeces was a way to extract extra nutrients from our food. Wolves often consume the droppings of their prey, which can contain partially digested plant matter and other goodies.

Others suggest it might be a way to supplement our diets with essential vitamins and minerals. Cat food is often higher in protein and fat than dog food, and their droppings can contain concentrated doses of these nutrients.

Then there's the idea that it's a scavenging behaviour, a way to make sure no potential food source goes to waste. We dogs are opportunistic eaters, after all. If it smells even remotely edible, we'll give it a shot.

Whatever the reason, I found myself irresistibly drawn to the cat litter tray. It was like a siren song, a pungent perfume that called to me from across the house. No sooner would my feline companions deposit a fresh offering than I'd come running, my nose twitching in anticipation.

My humans, of course, were less than thrilled with my new hobby.

"Ben, no!" the mistress would shout, lunging for me as I made a beeline for the litter box. "Drop it! Drop it right now!"

But I was too quick for her. I'd dart in, snatch up my prize, and be gone before she could lay a hand on me. I'd hide under the dining room table or behind the couch, savouring my ill-gotten gains with a connoisseur's relish.

The master tried to thwart me by moving the litter tray to a different room, somewhere he thought I wouldn't find it. But he underestimated the power of a determined dog's nose. No matter where he hid it—bedroom, bathroom, even the utility room—I always managed to sniff it out.

Next, they attempted to block my access with a baby gate. They figured if they could keep me from getting to the litter tray, I'd eventually lose interest and move on to less disgusting pastimes.

Oh, how naive they were.

The first time I encountered the gate, I was momentarily stymied. But then I noticed that the fixings were not secure enough, and I managed to push my way past the barrier and into the room beyond. The gate dropped to the floor with a clang as I dived for those sought-after nuggets.

The mistress heard the clatter and found me there a few minutes later, my head buried in the litter tray, my tail wagging in ecstasy.

"Ben!" she cried, her voice a mix of horror and disbelief. "How did you . . .? Never mind, just get out of there!"

She shooed me away, but the damage was done. I'd had my fix, and I was already plotting my next move.

This went on for weeks. No matter what obstacles my humans put in my path, I always found a way around them. It was like a game of cat and mouse . . . if the mouse was a labrador with an insatiable appetite for feline faeces.

Finally, in desperation, they resorted to drastic measures. They went out and bought a new kind of litter tray, one that was completely enclosed except for a small hole in the top. The idea was that the cats could jump in and out, but I wouldn't be able to reach the contents.

I remember the day they brought it home, so proud of their clever solution. They set it up in the usual spot, filled it with fresh litter, and stood back to admire their handiwork.

"There," the master said, dusting off his hands. "Let's see him get into that."

Ember approached the new tray warily, sniffing at it from all angles. She seemed a bit perplexed by the setup, but after a bit of investigation, she figured out the drill. Ember hopped up, wriggled through the hole, and did her business.

I watched from a distance, my heart sinking. It seemed my days of litter diving were over. The tray was like a little fortress, impenetrable to my questing snout. I circled it a few times, looking for weaknesses, but it was no use. The humans had won.

Much as it pained me to admit it, they had finally outsmarted me. The litter tray was now truly off-limits, a forbidden zone I could only dream about.

But here's the thing: even though I couldn't indulge my craving anymore, I never really lost the taste for it. Even now, years later, I still sometimes catch a whiff of cat droppings on the breeze and feel a stirring of longing in my gut.

It's a part of who I am, I suppose. A remnant of my wild heritage, a link to my ancestral past. And while I may have given up the habit, I'll never forget the thrill of the hunt, the satisfaction of the score.

So if you ever catch your dog with their nose in the litter box, don't be too hard on them. They're not being naughty or disobedient. They're just following their instincts, indulging a craving that's hardwired into their DNA.

And who knows? Maybe one day, science will come up with a way to make cat poo safe and nutritious for canine consumption. Stranger things have happened.

But until then, I suppose I'll just have to content myself with the occasional surreptitious sniff...and the memories of a time when the world was my litter box, and every day was a delicious adventure.

The Puddle Plunderer

There's something about a good puddle that just calls to a dog's soul. It's like a siren song, a temptation that cannot be resisted. And let me tell you, I was no exception to this canine truth.

It was a dreary day in the park, the kind of grey, drizzly affair that so often descends upon our little corner of England. The master had bundled up in his coat and boots, prepared for the inevitable mud and muck. I, of course, had no such protection, my fur already slicked to my body in anticipation of the delights to come.

Binx trotted alongside us, his expression one of mild curiosity. This was his first time joining us on a walk in such conditions, and he had no idea of the chaos that was about to unfold.

As we entered the field, I could barely contain my excitement. The grass was dotted with shimmering pools of water, each one a miniature oasis calling out to be explored. I strained against my leash, eager to be set free.

The master, in a moment of distraction, unclipped my lead. It was only as he watched me bolt towards the nearest puddle that the realisation dawned on him: he had forgotten about my affinity for big, dirty puddles, and now it was too late to stop me.

"Ben, no!" he cried, but his words were lost in the patter of the rain and the thunder of my paws.

I hit the puddle at full speed, water spraying up in a glorious arc around me. Oh, the bliss of it! The cool, muddy water splashing my belly, the squelch of the muck between my toes. I was in heaven, lost in a world of sensory delight.

Binx, who had been watching from the sidelines, let out a startled meow. His eyes were wide, his tail puffed up to twice its normal size. He had never seen anything like this before, and he wasn't quite sure what to make of it.

"What on earth is he doing?" he demanded, turning to the master with an accusatory glare.

The master sighed, running a hand down his face. "He's being a labrador," he said wearily. "A very muddy, very enthusiastic labrador."

I paid them no mind, too caught up in my puddle-jumping bliss. I pranced and splashed, my tail wagging up a storm. I ducked my head under the water, blowing bubbles and snapping at the droplets. I was a dog possessed, a creature of pure, unbridled joy.

Binx watched in horror as I cavorted through the muck, his fastidious feline sensibilities thoroughly offended. "Make him stop!" he yowled, backing away from the edge of the puddle. "He's making a complete idiot of himself!"

The master, perhaps realising the futility of trying to rein me in, just shook his head. "You get used to the mess after a while," the master said.

But Binx was not to be placated. He paced back and forth at the edge of the puddle, his tail lashing in agitation. "Used to it?" he spat. "I will never get used to this. It's gross . . . it's . . . it's . . ." He trailed off, seemingly at a loss for words.

I paused in my revelry to grin at him, my tongue lolling out of the side of my mouth. "It's fun!" I barked, sending up another spray of water. "Come on in, Binx! The water's fine!"

Binx recoiled as if I'd suggested he take a bath in a sewer. "Absolutely not," he hissed. "I am a cat, Ben. We do not wallow in filth. It's not cool."

I just laughed, too happy to be offended. "Suit yourself," I panted, turning my attention back to the glorious muck. "More for me, then!"

And with that, I launched myself into the next puddle, sending up a wave of muddy water that nearly drenched poor Binx. He yowled in indignation, leaping back with a hiss.

The master, taking pity on the bedraggled feline, scooped him up and tucked him inside his coat. "There, there," he soothed, trying to hide a smile. "You're safe now. The big bad puddle can't get you."

Binx just glared balefully out at me from the safety of his new perch, his eyes narrowed to slits. I could almost hear him plotting his revenge, dreaming up ways to get back at me for subjecting him to such indignities.

But I was too far gone to care. I was in my element, a creature of mud and muck and unbridled joy. This was what life was all about, wasn't it? These little pockets of pure, unfiltered happiness. The chance to let loose and be your true, messy self, consequences be damned.

And so I cavorted and splashed, blissfully unaware of the exasperated looks being exchanged between the master and Binx. Let them judge, I thought. Let them shake their heads and mutter about the state of my fur. I knew the truth—that there was magic in these moments, a pure, unadulterated bliss that couldn't be found anywhere else.

Finally, after what felt like hours of glorious, mucky playtime, the master managed to corral me, clipping my leash back on and leading me out of the park. I trotted happily alongside him, my fur caked with mud, my tail still wagging with the joy of it all.

Binx, who had been released from the confines of the master's coat, walked a few paces ahead of us, his tail held high in the air. He kept shooting me disgusted looks over his shoulder, as if he couldn't quite believe the state of me.

"You're filthy," he sniffed, wrinkling his nose. "Absolutely filthy. How can you stand it?"

I just grinned at him, my tongue lolling out of the side of my mouth. "It's not so bad," I panted. "You should try it sometime, Binx. Might loosen you up a bit."

Binx looked horrified at the very suggestion. "I would rather lick a cactus," he said primly. "Cats are clean creatures, Ben. We take pride in our appearance. Not like you dogs, rolling around in every bit of muck you can find."

I was about to retort when the master interrupted us, his voice stern. "Right," he said, looking down at me with a mix of exasperation and resignation. "You know what this means, don't you, Ben?"

My tail stopped wagging. I did know. It meant the dreaded B-word. Bath.

I tried to look as pitiful as possible as the master led me into the house, hoping against hope that he might take pity on me and let me off the hook just this once. But it was no use.

He was already filling up the tub, the sound of running water a death knell to my muddy bliss.

Binx, of course, found the whole thing hilarious. He perched himself on the edge of the sink, his eyes glinting with malicious glee as he watched the master wrestle me into the tub.

"Oh, how the mighty have fallen," he purred, his tail swishing back and forth. "The great Ben, reduced to a whimpering mess at the sight of a little soap and water."

I glared at him as the master began to scrub me down, the warm water sluicing away the mud and grime. It wasn't that I hated baths, exactly. I just hated the indignity of it all. A dog of my stature, subjected to such humiliations? It was almost too much to bear.

But the master was relentless, lathering me up from head to tail until I was a sudsy, bedraggled mess. Binx watched the whole thing with a smirk on his face, clearly relishing my discomfort.

"Not so fun now, is it?" he said smugly. "Maybe next time you'll think twice before diving into every muddy puddle you see."

I just grumbled under my breath, too miserable to come up with a proper retort. The master, perhaps sensing my distress, tried to soothe me with gentle words and scratchies behind the ears. But it was no use. I was a dog betrayed, a noble beast brought low by the cruel whims of fate and my so called feline best friend.

Finally, after what felt like an eternity, the master deemed me clean enough and lifted me out of the tub. I stood there, shivering, and pathetic, as he towelled me off, my fur sticking up in every direction.

Binx, who had grown bored of watching my suffering, had wandered off to find a cosy spot for a nap. I could hear him purring contentedly from the living room, no doubt dreaming of a world without muddy dogs and their messy antics.

As the master finished drying me off, I couldn't help but feel a twinge of resentment. It wasn't fair, I thought. Why did cats get to stay clean and dry, while dogs were forced to endure the indignities of the bath? Why were we judged for our love of mud and muck, while they were praised for their prissy fastidiousness?

But then I remembered the joy of the puddles, the sheer, unbridled bliss of being a dog in the moment. And I realised that I wouldn't trade it for anything, not even a lifetime of spotless fur and smug feline superiority.

Because that's what being a dog is all about, isn't it? Embracing the mess, the chaos, the sheer, unadulterated joy of living life to the fullest. And if that means a few extra baths along the way? Well, that's just the price we pay for being the most magnificent creatures on earth.

So let the cats have their cleanliness, their dainty little paws, and their delicate sensibilities. I'll take the mud and the muck and the glorious, messy chaos of being a dog any day.

And as for Binx? Well, he may never understand the appeal of a good puddle. But that's okay. He's got his own brand of feline magic, his own way of finding joy in the world. And together, we make quite the pair—the prissy puss and the muddy mutt, two unlikely friends navigating the ups and downs of life with our own unique style.

And I wouldn't have it any other way.

A Raisin for Concern

It was a bank holiday, the perfect excuse for the master's brother and sister-in-law to extend their visit an extra day. Their weekend with us had been a lively affair, full of fun and games, especially with April and Cameron around to liven things up.

As the family prepared to head home later that afternoon, they lingered in the living room, reluctant to leave just yet. April sat cuddled up on the settee with her mum, munching away on a small box of raisins while the grown-ups chatted.

I loved having the kids around. They had such a zest for life, an energy that matched my own doggy joie de vivre. Plus, they were always good for a sneaky treat or two when the grown-ups weren't looking.

So there I was, sprawled out on the rug nearby, my tail thumping contentedly as I kept one eye on April and her raisin box. Cameron, on the other hand, hung back a bit, his nose twitching as he eyed me warily. It wasn't until later that I found out about his pet allergy, a condition that made being around furry critters like myself a bit of a challenge.

As I understand it, pet allergies are caused by a reaction to proteins in an animal's skin cells, saliva, or urine. For someone with an allergy, breathing in those particles can trigger their immune system to release chemicals that cause symptoms like sneezing, itchy eyes, and even trouble breathing.

Cameron's parents had come prepared, giving him medication before the visit to help keep his allergies under control. Without it, I overheard them explaining, he could end up quite miserable. But even with the meds, Cameron seemed to prefer keeping his distance, joining in the fun from afar.

It was all going smoothly enough until the Raisin Incident. One minute, April was happily snacking away on the settee. The next, I heard a rustle of plastic and a small gasp. Looking up, I saw a look of horror on April's face as a single raisin tumbled from the box and landed right by my nose.

Now, here's the thing about raisins and dogs: they don't mix. In fact, they can be downright dangerous. Grapes and raisins contain a toxin that can cause kidney failure in canines, and even a small amount can make a dog seriously ill.

Of course, I didn't know any of this at the time. All I knew was that there was a tasty-looking morsel on the floor, and I was a labrador with a one-track mind when it came to food. Before April's mum could stop me, I'd snarfed up the raisin, swallowing it down with a satisfied gulp just as the mistress walked into the room with some drinks and let out a yelp of dismay. There was a flurry of activity as she called out to the master—bless him—who wasted no time. He whisked me off to the vet, a grim expression on his face as he explained the situation over the phone. It was a bank holiday, which meant our usual practice was closed, but they directed us to an emergency vet and out-of-hours service that was open.

I could tell the master was worried sick. I tried to reassure him with a few licks to the hand, but I was feeling a bit off myself. My stomach was starting to churn, and I had a nasty feeling that this wasn't going to end well.

At the practice, they gave me something to make me vomit, a thoroughly unpleasant experience that left me heaving and shaking, my tail tucked between my legs.

But it did the trick. Up came the raisin . . . along with two others that April hadn't even realised she'd dropped and I'd eaten. The vet explained that I was lucky that they'd caught it in time before any serious damage could be done. But it was a close call, and a sobering reminder of just how fragile we dogs can be.

The whole ordeal ended up costing the master a pretty penny—two hundred and fifty pounds to be exact. It was a lot of money, especially for a simple mistake like a dropped raisin. But the master never complained, not once. He was just happy to have me home safe and sound, even if I was a bit worse for wear.

I tried my best to be a good sport about it all, to show them that I was still the same old Ben, ready and raring for a game of fetch or a belly rub. But even I had to admit, I was feeling a bit sorry for myself. It's no fun being the centre of attention when it's for all the wrong reasons.

It had been an eventful few days, full of ups and downs and unexpected detours. But that's life, isn't it? You never know what's going to happen next, be it a surprise visit or a stray raisin . . . or two.

The important thing is to roll with the punches, to find the joy in the chaos and the love during the madness. And if there's one thing I'm good at, it's finding joy. It's the labrador way, after all.

Ben's Big Adventure

It was a perfect spring afternoon and I was outside playing with my best buddy Binx in the back garden. I threw my favourite ball up in the air and then I would watch it fall and roll away before I bounded after it and snatched it up in my jaws. But Binx suddenly darting in front of me, his sleek black fur shimmering in the sunlight, made me pause what I was doing.

"Hey, look at this!" he meowed excitedly. "The gate's open. Let's go explore!"

I hesitated, glancing back at the house. "I don't know, Binx . . . We're supposed to stay in the garden."

Binx flicked his tail mischievously. "Oh come on, where's your sense of adventure? It'll be fun! We won't go far, promise."

Unable to resist, I followed Binx as he squeezed through the unlatched gate. My tail wagged with nervous excitement as we trotted down the garden path side by side and emerged onto the footpath. So many new sights and smells!

We ambled along, sniffing every lamppost and shrub. Then Binx spotted a lush grassy hill. "Race you to the top!" he yowled, taking off at a sprint.

I chased after him, my legs pumping. At the crest of the hill, we tumbled onto the soft grass, panting, and laughing. We romped and wrestled, the warm sun on our fur. I loved this cat, he was such a good playmate!

"Would you look at that?" remarked a passing jogger, shaking her head in amazement at the sight of a dog and cat frolicking together.

We played until we were happily tired out. "We should probably head home," I said, remembering my duty.

Binx nodded. "Good idea. Mistress will be missing us."

We made our way back, retracing our steps. As we scurried up the drive the front door opened and the mistress emerged with my leash in hand, ready to come retrieve us. She blinked in astonishment to see us already home.

"There you two escape artists are! I was worried!"

Binx and I exchanged a glance and I gave her my best winsome doggy grin, my tongue lolling. We were both happily tired from our secret adventure, not guilty in the slightest.

My mistress just shook her head and smiled. "What am I going to do with you rascals? Well, I'm glad you had fun and made it home safe. Let's get you some water. You look parched!"

As I lapped up the cool water beside Binx, I decided that having a cat for a best friend was the best thing in the world. I couldn't wait for our next adventure, just the two of us.

Walking the Walk

The mistress hadn't been herself lately. Her usual boundless energy was flagging, weighed down by fatigue and discomfort from the sweltering summer heat. Gone were the days of her bounding through the kitchen, whipping up culinary masterpieces with ease. Now, just mustering the strength to stand over the stove left her drained and wilted like a flower deprived of water.

That meant more responsibilities fell on the master's shoulders. He rose before dawn to take me out for my morning constitutionals, then rushed off to his work, only to return hours later and immediately don the chef's hat. It would be well into the night by the time he'd prepared the evening meal and we would eat as a family.

I could see the toll it was taking. The master's eyes grew ringed with exhaustion, his shoulders slumping wearily as he trudged from task to task. But he refused to complain, stubbornly insisting he could manage. That was my master: steadfast and self-sacrificing to the end.

"Niall, this can't go on," the mistress fretted one night as we lingered over the dinner dishes. "You're going to run yourself into the ground at this rate."

The master tried to wave her off with a placating smile. "It's nothing I can't handle, love."

He reached down to tousle my ears affectionately. I tried to match his bravado with a raucous tail-wag, but couldn't quite hide my concern. As the days wore on, I could see him dragging more and more.

"But that's just it!" The mistress set down her plate with a clatter. "You're taking on too much with the walks, the cooking, your work. We need an extra pair of hands around here before one of us ends up in hospital."

An idea seemed to strike her then, and she turned to me with rekindled determination. "What we need is a dog walker to take some of the burden off you during the day."

And so began the great dog walker search. The master and mistress pored over adverts and conducted numerous telephone interviews, vetting each candidate as thoroughly as if they were applying to be the Queen's personal butler.

"You can never be too careful," the master insisted. "We need to find someone trustworthy."

At last, they settled on a likely candidate—a cheery middle-aged woman with decades of dog handling experience under her belt. Sue had all the proper documentation, from pet first-aid certifications to a litany of glowing reviews from former clients. More importantly, she passed my most critical sniff test with flying colours.

After a few introductory visits for us to get acquainted, Sue arrived bright and early one morning to embark on her first official dog walk with yours truly.

"Now Ben, you be a good boy for Miss Sue," the master instructed, scratching behind my ears. "No leading her on a merry chase, you hear? I'm counting on you to mind your manners."

I barked dutifully and allowed Sue to slip on my lead. So far, so good.

What happened next, however, was a series of misadventures that would have made even the most seasoned dog walker throw up her hands in defeat. From the moment she collected me in her pooch mobile, it was as if some unseen force had possessed me, stoking the fires of my primal canine instincts.

At the sight of the other dogs joining me on my walk, something stirred within me. Unbidden, my body reacted on pure animal impulse, rear hiking, and everything else positioning for...well, you know, stud or bitch, it did not matter. Before Sue could react, I was hunched and humping away at the bewildered mutts like a dog possessed.

"Ben! Heel! Down boy!" Sue barked in abject horror, struggling to disentangle me from my poor, traumatised victims. But I was utterly single-minded in my pursuit, oblivious to her frantic commands as I seized every opportunity for male supremacy.

With a strength born of sheer mortification, she finally wrenched me free and bundled me away in shame, my tail tucked firmly between my legs. Our walk didn't last much longer after that, the mood rather soured.

Back home, Sue wasted no time setting the record straight.

"I'm sorry Kirsty," she addressed the mistress, "but I simply can't walk Ben anymore. His . . . arousal issues are more than I can handle. I've never seen such flagrant humping in all my years!"

The mistress could only nod weakly, too embarrassed to meet Sue's gaze.

"I understand completely. Thank you for your time."

With that, the dog walker beat a hasty retreat, no doubt eager to put as much distance as possible between herself and my overactive libido.

Now, I know what you're thinking—how could a neutered pooch like me still be chasing tail (any tail, for that matter) with such relentless ardour? Well, as it turns out, even stripped of the biological imperative, some dogs just can't shake those frisky urges. Call it a phantom itch that needs scratching, if you will.

Humping behaviour is perfectly normal for us canines, a hard-wired residual mating instinct that can be triggered by anything from anxiety to sheer exuberance. Of course, that's little comfort when your beloved pet is going to town on an innocent bystander right there on the footpath!

With the professional dog walker option officially a bust, the master knew he needed another solution, and fast. As the mistress's condition persisted, his own energy reserves were becoming dangerously depleted.

That's when he turned to Bronwyn and Jacob.

"Kids, I need to ask a huge favour of you both," he began one evening, weariness etching his features. "With your mum poorly, the dog walks are really doing a number on me between work and running the house. I could use an extra set of hands, just until things settle down around here."

Bronwyn and Jacob exchanged sceptical looks, their lingering apprehension towards going out in all weathers and disconnecting from their gaming visible. I aimed my most winsome pant in their direction, eyes rounded beseechingly.

"Do we have to?" Bronwyn asked.

"Just a quick circuit around the block, no more than that. I wouldn't ask if I wasn't desperate," the master reassured.

They wavered, their youthful apathy slowly melting beneath the master's plaintive plea. With matching grudging nods, they accepted the burden.

And that's how I found myself on a rotating schedule of walks not just with the master, but Bronwyn and Jacob too. Sure, they grumbled and groused every step of the way, but I could sense the reluctant affection simmering beneath. Each time I bounded back into the house after our jaunt, I was rewarded with belly rubs and begrudging head scratches.

It wasn't easy on any of us. Coordinating the walks was a logistical nightmare at times. But we muddled through, one outing at a time, slowly finding our rhythm as a team.

If there's one thing I've learned over the years, it's that the human concept of "family" extends far beyond just breed and blood. It's a bond forged from shared struggles, of circling the wagons when the going gets tough and standing united against whatever the world throws your way.

In those days of extra responsibilities, we became a pack—the master, the mistress, Bronwyn, Jacob, and me. We took turns leading and following, stumbling at times, but always catching each other when we faltered.

Because that's what family does. We have each other's backs, putting aside our differences for the greater good. We weather every storm together, paw in hand, one step at a time.

And if I happened to slip up and attempt to hump a stray mutt in the process? Well, they knew by now that I meant no harm. I was simply walking the walk, living my truth as naturally as any dog could.

No judgments, no lectures. Just the master's resigned sigh and a gentle redirection back to more appropriate behaviour.

That's the beauty of being part of a real pack. They let you be you, quirks, and all, secure in the knowledge that your loyalty is unconditional. And for a canine like me, what could be better than that?

Diary of a Humper: Operation Sniff 'n Scatter

"Sit," the mistress commanded in a firm tone as she pointed to the floor. I happily plopped my rump down, tongue lolling out happily. Treats on the horizon? Don't mind if I do!

She offered an approving scratch behind the ears. "Good boy, Ben. Now we have a special guest coming over to help with some . . . obedience matters."

My tail started thumping excitedly. A guest? For me? This was shaping up to be an excellent day already! Though, her cryptic tone did have me momentarily pondering what possible "matters" she could mean.

The doorbell rang, and suddenly the answer came bounding through in the form of a wiry, energetic woman with a sunshine smile. But it wasn't her arrival that gave me paws—it was the veritable Mary Poppins carpet bag she was lugging, stuffed to bursting with an intriguing array of doodads and rascally ruffs.

"Thanks for coming over, Nicky," the mistress began once we were all situated in the living room. "As I mentioned, we've been having some . . . issues . . . with Ben's social behaviour around other dogs lately."

The woman—Nicky, apparently—laughed in a bright, musical way as I immediately rolled over and presented my belly in the universally recognised "rub me!" pose. "Oh, I can already tell this fella is just a sweetheart!" She leaned down to afford me a good scratching. "Though I suspect I know what particular 'issue' you might be referring to."

"The humping," my mistress said with a sigh. "He just doesn't seem to understand it's not . . . appropriate public behaviour."

Aha! So that was what we were there to discuss. I flicked an ear in mild embarrassment as I recalled my more recent faux pas and the very stern lecture I had received from the mistress.

In my defence, how was a healthy hound like me supposed to resist leaving my calling card on every patch of canine beauty I encountered? Spreading pivotal scent markers and assertions of virility is simply what us males do! Though I suppose the repeated a-hunching and slobbery face licking maybe took things a tad too far...

Nicky gave a conspiratorial wink as she reached into her bag of semi-miraculous holding. With a dramatic flourish, she produced a plush, oblong . . . thing. It appeared to be a bright blue hippo at first sniff, until she squished it between her palms and it released a heavenly, mouthwatering aroma.

"The answer to many undesirable doggy behaviours is simply making their minds work a little harder," she explained, rolling the peculiar squeaky chew toy my way. "In Ben's case, we're going to redirect that excessive . . . energy . . . into more positive outlets!"

I instantly abandon all pretences of being a dignified mature fellow. My paws danced in excitement as I barked feverishly, frothing at the prospect of getting that incredibly bacon-y smelling thing between my jaws. Nicky laughed again merrily, straightening up and giving me a few obedience commands before relinquishing her tantalising prize.

Over the next hour or so, she deftly walked us through a variety of interactive toys, scented games and clever reward-based exercises involving lots of jumping, stretching, and puzzle-solving for me. The whole time, I was panting up a storm, endorphins thundering through my veins in a glorious doggy session frenzy. Every time I mastered one of her challenges, I was showered with a veritable torrent of crunchies and scratches-behind-ears.

"You see how it works?" Nicky explained as I galloped in delirious circles, drunk on all the cerebral stimulation. "Lots of mental focus and energy burned in positive outlets. By the time a walk rolls around, he'll be so tired out from using his natural instincts for sniffing and foraging that any ... other ... instincts won't even occur to him!"

The mistress was positively beaming at the sheer simple genius of it all, hanging on Nicky's every word.

"Okay then, lay it on me woof-ness! What else have you got in that magical portable dog park of yours?"

Well, apart from those heady aromatics and puzzle feeders (seriously, who knew unbuckling a clasp could be SO rewarding?), Nicky also had some brilliant outdoorsy ideas to ensure my daily constitutionals were more scintillating than simple dawdling and squatting.

"It's all about making him WORK for his meals on those walks, kicking his foraging instincts into high gear," she says, producing a shiny silver pouch from her bounty of goodies.

"Load this up with extra smelly treats or even pieces of his kibble—whatever drives him completely muttonal."

My ears perked up and my nose started quivering in anticipation. Was she implying what I thought she was implying...?

"Then as you're strolling along, use the outdoor terrain to your advantage!" Nicky bundled us all outside for a live demonstration. She started scattering the irresistible treats concentrates along in a meandering path through some shrubs and then continuing to the grassy park verge opposite. "A few in one spot here, a couple more over there beneath that bench. Just get Ben's nose engaged and focused on constantly hunting those delicious morsels!"

I was already anxiously prancing from foot to foot like I had a pocket full of bees. At the mistress's cue of "Go sniff!" I absolutely bounded forth in a flurry paws, my mind completely consumed by the possibility of delectable treasures hidden everywhere.

Nose to the ground, I zigzagged like a delirious minesweeper drone from one scent patch to the next. When I finally located each jackpot of treats, I honed in like a Terminator while scarfing them down with ravenous chomps and hoovering licks. Somewhere in the distance, I vaguely registered the mistress's squeals of glee and Nicky's congratulatory praises. But my complete focus was immersed in the Hunt, the greatest game of all.

In fact, by the time the master whistled me back into a semi-orderly heel, my snout was slightly caked in grass and drool and my tongue was lolling out with exhausted satisfaction. All that mental and physical exertion, chasing invisible scent trails, negotiating tricky terrain while obsessively questing and strategizing . . . Why, I felt more fulfilled and gloriously tuckered out than if we'd simply done laps around the park!

"You see what a difference it makes to his temperament?" Nicky proclaimed while towelling off my sloppy muzzle. "He'll be so pleasantly zoned now that other dogs will be the last thing on his mind. You can count on that!"

All I could manage was a wheezy pant that hopefully translated to immense gratitude for this revolutionary way of making my walk times more . . . substantial. My primitive hunting instincts felt thoroughly slaked, blissed out in lingering beta wave stupor.

Sure enough, later that day as the master and I ventured out for our customary neighbourhood amblings, my only focus was feverishly devouring every redirected path and target box of scrumptious leavings, snuffling in deep trances and flinging my whole body into shrubby thickets to hoover up every crumb. I was so single-mindedly fixated on sniffing out my earthly rewards that even a pert little dog tail doesn't register a blip.

Huh . . . who knew the solution to curbing my "over-enthusiastic" social urges was simply making me work that big, beautiful nose more?

Sure, I could still happily chase squirrels and roll in mud until the cows come home, but the prospect of openly flirting with every furball on four legs somehow lost its appeal. At least for now.

As for the master, he spent the entire trek back beaming and singing the praises of their new canine guru. "Honestly, where has Nicky been all Ben's life? We're making this part of our routine from now on!"

Music to my deliriously flapping ears. For now, whenever those old amorous tendencies try creeping back, I'd simply flash a wistful gaze to wherever those heavenly scented treats awaited . . . and instantly be swept back into cerebral cravings of the purest kind.

Sure beat getting scolded all the time. At least this approach helped keep my focus where it really belonged . . . playing the hunt, mastering new tricks, relishing each glorious new day of walkies with my true love and partner forever, the mere sight of whom, I'm more than proud to admit, gets my tail wagging harder than any dalliance ever could.

A Tale of Unlikely Heroics

Life, as any seasoned canine philosopher will tell you, has a way of testing our mettle when we least expect it. Just when you think you've got everything figured out, the universe throws you a curveball that sends you scrambling to redefine the very essence of who you are and what you're capable of.

For me, that moment of reckoning came on what had started as a perfectly ordinary afternoon stroll with my feline compatriot, Binx.

Now, I know what you're thinking—a dog and a cat, out for a leisurely constitutional together? Surely that's the stuff of fairy tales and cheesy greeting cards. But Binx and I had long since transcended the traditional boundaries of species rivalry, forging a friendship as unlikely as it was unshakeable.

Our daily walks had become something of a ritual, a chance for both of us to stretch our legs and indulge in a bit of neighbourhood gossip (well, more me doing the gossiping and Binx offering the occasional sardonic meow in response). We had our route down to a science, a carefully curated tour of all the best sniffing spots and sunbathing perches our little corner of the world had to offer.

But on this day, as we rounded the corner onto Maple Street, something was decidedly amiss. There was a charge in the air, a prickling sense of unease that sent my hackles rising and my tail tucking instinctively between my legs.

And then I saw it—the gaping maw of Mrs. Pemberton's side gate, left carelessly ajar like a yawning portal to some unknown chaos.

Now, it's worth noting that Mrs. Pemberton was the proud (if somewhat oblivious) owner of a massive brute of a dog named Brutus. A Rottweiler-Mastiff mix with more muscle than sense, Brutus had long been the terror of the neighbourhood's smaller furry residents.

I had always given the Pemberton place a wide berth on our walks, steering Binx clear of those imposing iron gates with a gentle nudge or a warning whine. But today, caught off-guard by the unexpected breach in our usual defences, I found myself frozen in place as the full implications of our predicament sank in.

Before I could so much as utter a warning bark, a dark blur came hurtling out of the open gate like a furry freight train. Brutus, in all his slobbering, snarling glory, had caught wind of our presence and was barrelling towards us with single-minded determination.

Time seemed to slow to a crawl as I watched the massive dog close the distance between us, his jaws snapping and his eyes wild with predatory glee. In that moment, every instinct in my body screamed at me to turn tail and run, to save my own skin and leave Binx to fend for himself.

But then I caught sight of my feline friend out of the corner of my eye, his sleek form a study in nonchalant grace as he sized up the situation. And something deep within me, some long-dormant well of courage I hadn't even known I possessed, suddenly roared to life.

With a growl that started low in my chest and built to a fearsome crescendo, I planted my paws firmly on the pavement and stood my ground. I might have been half Brutus's size, a genteel family pet more accustomed to belly rubs than brawls, but in that moment I was a force to be reckoned with.

"Run, Binx!" I barked, my voice rough with a mixture of fear and determination. "I'll hold him off!"

But Binx, true to his feline nature, had already formulated a far more elegant solution to our predicament. With a graceful leap that would have put an Olympic gymnast to shame, he sailed effortlessly onto the nearest fence post and settled in to watch the proceedings with an air of amused detachment.

Left to face the oncoming canine juggernaut on my own, I did the only thing I could think of—I charged. With a yowl that was equal parts battle cry and terror, I hurled myself at Brutus with every ounce of strength I could muster.

What ensued was less an epic clash of titans and more a comedic dance of mismatched opponents. I darted and weaved, nipping at Brutus's heels and barking furiously to distract him from his original feline quarry. Brutus, for his part, seemed more bewildered than aggressive, clearly unprepared for prey that fought back with such tenacity.

Around and around the cul-de-sac we went, a whirling dervish of fur and slobber and increasingly exhausted panting. I could hear the shouts of the master attempting to put an end to this impromptu circus act.

And through it all, there was Binx, perched serenely atop his fence post like some feline deity deigning to observe the chaos of us mere mortals. Every so often he would let out a disinterested "mrow," as if to say, "Oh, do get on with it, you ridiculous creatures."

Just when I thought my legs might give out from sheer exhaustion, salvation arrived in the form of Mrs. Pemberton herself. With a shrill whistle and a shouted command that could have curdled milk, she brought Brutus to a screeching halt.

"Brutus! Heel! Bad dog!" she screeched, her face as red as her impeccably manicured nails. "I am so sorry, I don't know how he got out. Are you alright, you poor thing?"

I collapsed onto the pavement in a heap of trembling limbs and heaving sides, too winded to even offer up a reassuring wag of my tail. But as Mrs. Pemberton fussed over me and Brutus skulked back to his yard with his tail between his legs, I felt a warm glow of pride begin to spread through my chest.

I had done it. Against all odds and my own deepest insecurities, I had stood up to the neighbourhood bully and emerged victorious. I had protected my friend (even if said friend had been in absolutely no danger whatsoever) and proven to myself that I was made of sterner stuff than I had ever imagined.

As if sensing the shift in my demeanour, Binx chose that moment to gracefully descend from his perch and saunter over to where I lay. With a gentle headbutt and a purr that seemed to vibrate through my very bones, he offered his own unique brand of feline gratitude.

"Not bad for an old dog," he seemed to say, his green eyes glinting with a mixture of amusement and genuine affection.

"Though next time, perhaps we could opt for a less dramatic afternoon constitutional?"

I couldn't help but huff out a laugh at that, the last of the adrenaline draining from my system and leaving me feeling oddly light and giddy. Because that was the thing about true friendship, wasn't it? It had a way of bringing out the very best in us, of pushing us to be braver and stronger and more resilient than we ever thought possible.

And as we made our way home, a little worse for wear but spirits high, I couldn't help but feel profoundly grateful for the unlikely bond that had brought us to this moment. Dog and cat, hero and damsel (though Binx would undoubtedly take umbrage at that particular designation), steadfast companions through thick and thin.

It might not have been the peaceful stroll we had set out for, but it had been an adventure for the ages. And really, isn't that what life is all about? The unexpected twists and turns, the moments of fear and triumph, and the unshakeable certainty that no matter what challenges we might face . . . we never have to face them alone.

So here's to unlikely friendships and unexpected acts of bravery. Here's to the Binxes of the world, who inspire us to be our best selves even as they drive us to the brink of madness. And here's to the knowledge that even the most ordinary of days can become extraordinary in the blink of an eye.

Because as long as we have each other to lean on and laugh with, to protect and be protected by, well . . . there's no telling what heights we might reach or what obstacles we might overcome.

And for this old dog, learning new tricks with every passing day, that's more than enough to keep my tail wagging and my heart full of hope for whatever adventures might lie just around the next corner.

An Unexpected Encounter

They say that lightning never strikes twice in the same place, but as I was about to discover on yet another seemingly innocuous afternoon stroll, the universe has a wry sense of humour when it comes to testing one's mettle.

It had been a few weeks since the Brutus incident, and I'd like to say I'd been strutting about the neighbourhood with a newfound air of canine confidence. In reality, I was still processing the adrenaline rush of my unexpected heroics, my daily walks with the master tinged with a mixture of pride and lingering nervousness.

On this day, we'd ventured a bit further afield than usual, lured by the promise of new scents and sights. The master, ever attuned to my moods, had sensed my need for a change of scenery and obligingly suggested we explore uncharted territory.

"Come on, old boy," he'd said with a fond smile, clipping on my lead. "Let's see what adventures await us today, shall we?"

If only we'd known just how prophetic those words would prove to be.

The pavement was a picturesque affair, all dappled sunlight and rustling leaves, the air thick with the heady perfume of wildflowers and loamy earth. I trotted along at the master's side, my nose working overtime to catalogue the myriad new scents assaulting my senses.

We'd just rounded a particularly sharp bend in the path, the thick hedgerows on either side creating a sort of green tunnel effect, when it happened. One moment we were alone in our pastoral idyll, and the next... chaos erupted.

From around the corner came a blur of motion and sound—a massive Alsatian, all sleek muscle and flashing teeth, barrelling towards us like a furry missile. Behind him, barely visible through the maelstrom of flying leaves and startled birdsong, was his human—a slight woman who looked about as prepared to handle her canine companion as I was to sprout wings and fly.

Time seemed to slow to a crawl as my brain frantically tried to process the unfolding scene. The Alsatian's eyes were locked on me, his powerful haunches bunching as he prepared to launch himself in my direction. The woman's voice, shrill with panic, cut through the air like a knife:

"Max! No! Heel!"

But Max, it seemed, had other ideas. With a spring that would have put an Olympic long jumper to shame, he hurled himself towards me in a flurry of fur and slobber.

Now, I'd like to say that my recent brush with bravery had imbued me with the courage of a lion, ready to face down this new threat with the same tenacity I'd shown with Brutus. The reality was somewhat less heroic.

With a yelp that was equal parts surprise and terror, I executed what can only be described as an undignified sideways scramble. My paws scrabbled for purchase on the loose gravel of the path as I ducked and weaved, driven by some primal instinct for self-preservation.

Max, caught off-guard by my unexpected evasive manoeuvres, sailed past me with a look of canine bewilderment. But his trajectory, no longer impeded by my furry bulk, now had him on a direct collision course with his own unsuspecting human.

What followed was a scene of such perfect slapstick comedy that, had I not been amid my own panic-induced fugue state, I might have appreciated for its cinematic quality.

The woman, already off-balance from being yanked along in Max's wake, caught the full brunt of her dog's considerable momentum. With a startled "Oof!" that seemed to echo through the suddenly silent lane, she went down in a tangle of limbs and lead, sprawling across the path like a felled tree.

For a moment, everything was still. The master, his hand still clutched tightly around my lead, stood frozen in place with his mouth agape. I cowered behind his legs, my tail tucked firmly between my legs and my ears pinned flat against my skull. And Max? He sat in the middle of the path, looking for all the world like he couldn't quite figure out how he'd ended up in this predicament.

It was the woman's groan that finally broke the spell of stunned silence.

"Oh, bloody hell," she muttered, pushing herself up onto her elbows with a wince. "Max, you great lummox, what am I going to do with you?"

The master snapped into action at the sound of distress. "Oh my goodness, are you alright?" he gasped, rushing forward to offer a helping hand. "That was quite a tumble you took!"

As the two humans fussed over scraped palms and bruised dignity, I found myself face to face with the cause of all this commotion. Max, his initial burst of exuberance seemingly spent, regarded me with an almost sheepish expression.

"Woof?" he offered tentatively, his tail giving a hopeful little wag.

And just like that, the last of my fear melted away, replaced by a grudging sense of canine solidarity. After all, hadn't I been in his paws not so long ago, caught up in the throes of excitement and causing no small amount of chaos?

With a dignified sniff that I hoped conveyed both forgiveness and a gentle admonishment, I cautiously extended my nose for a proper greeting. Max, eager to make amends, responded with enthusiasm, and soon we were engaged in the time-honoured ritual of mutual bottom-sniffing.

By the time our humans had sorted themselves out, dusting off clothes and exchanging rueful laughs over the follies of dog ownership, Max and I had reached a tentative truce. We might not have been bosom buddies, but we'd found common ground in the shared experience of being, well, dogs—creatures of impulse and enthusiasm, forever keeping our humans on their toes.

As we parted ways, the master and I continuing our walk while Max and his somewhat battered owner headed back the way they'd come, I couldn't help but reflect on the strange and wonderful unpredictability of life.

Here I was, still basking in the afterglow of my heroic stand against Brutus, only to be reminded of my own vulnerability in the face of unexpected challenges. It was a humbling experience, to be sure, but also a strangely comforting one.

Because that's the thing about life, isn't it? It's full of twists and turns, moments of triumph and moments of terror, often coming when we least expect them. But it's in navigating those unexpected encounters, those moments that push us out of our comfort zones, that we truly grow and learn.

So here's to the Maxes of the world, the chaos-bringers who keep us on our toes and remind us not to take ourselves too seriously. Here's to the masters who stand by us through thick and thin, offering a steadying hand and a reassuring word when we need it most.

And most of all, here's to the resilience of the canine spirit—that ineffable quality that allows us to bounce back from even the most undignified of tumbles, tails wagging and spirits high.

Because at the end of the day, isn't that what being a dog is all about? Living in the moment, embracing the unexpected, and always being ready for the next big adventure ... even if it comes barrelling around a blind corner when we least expect it.

A Feline Fracas

They say that truth is often stranger than fiction, but even I, a dog who's seen his fair share of peculiar happenings, was unprepared for the bizarre turn our daily constitutional was about to take.

It was a crisp autumn morning, the air tinged with the subtle perfume of fallen leaves and wood smoke. The master had decided that Binx and I were both in need of a bit of fresh air and exercise, so we found ourselves embarking on what was meant to be a peaceful ramble through the local park.

Now, I should preface this by saying that Binx and I had long since established a sort of détente when it came to our shared outings. He would saunter along at his own pace, alternating between imperious struts and lazy meandering, while I trotted faithfully at the master's side. It was an arrangement that suited us all just fine, a delicate balance of feline independence and canine loyalty.

But on this morning, there was a restless energy crackling in the air, a sense of impending mischief that set my whiskers twitching with unease.

We had just rounded the bend near the old oak tree, its gnarled branches stretching out over the path like arthritic fingers, when we encountered another dog and its human. The dog, a stocky bulldog with a face only a mother could love, was ambling along without a care in the world, its jowls flapping with each wheezing breath.

Under normal circumstances, this would have been a non-event. A brief sniff of greeting, perhaps a perfunctory bark or two, and we'd all be on our merry way. But Binx, it seemed, had other ideas.

Before any of us could react, he had launched himself from his perch atop a nearby fence post, transforming in mid-air from a lazy house cat into a whirling dervish of claws and fur. He landed squarely on the bulldog's broad back, yowling like a banshee and swatting at the poor beast's ears with a ferocity that left us all slack-jawed in disbelief.

The bulldog, understandably startled by this unexpected aerial assault, let out a yelp that was equal parts surprise and indignation. It began to spin in frantic circles, trying in vain to dislodge its feline attacker, while its human danced around the melee, arms flailing uselessly.

"Binx!" the master cried, his voice a mixture of horror and disbelief. "What on earth has gotten into you? Stop that this instant!"

But Binx, caught up in the throes of whatever madness had seized him, paid him no heed. With a deft move that spoke of years of practice wrangling unruly felines, the master managed to pluck Binx from his perch and tuck him securely under one arm.

The bulldog's owner, red-faced and puffing almost as much as his beleaguered pet, rounded on us with a look of righteous indignation.

"What kind of irresponsible pet owner are you?" he bellowed, his moustache quivering with each word. "You need to keep that . . . that monster on a leash! He could have seriously hurt my dog!"

I stared at the two of them in utter bewilderment, clearly struggling to process both the absurdity of the situation and the man's outrageous accusation.

The master, however, was having none of it. His eyebrows shot up towards his hairline as he regarded the still-fuming bulldog owner with a mixture of amusement and incredulity.

"Now, hold on just a moment," he said, his voice taking on that dangerously calm tone that I knew preceded some of his most cutting remarks. "Are you seriously suggesting that we should have anticipated our house cat turning into a furry guided missile and attacking your dog? Perhaps we should invest in a feline straitjacket for our future outings?"

The sarcasm in his voice was thick enough to spread on toast, but it seemed to sail right over the head of our aggrieved accuser.

"Well . . . yes!" the man spluttered, his face growing even redder. "That's exactly what I'm saying! A responsible pet owner would never allow such a vicious creature to roam freely!"

At this, even I couldn't suppress a snort of disbelief. Vicious creature? Binx? The same cat who spent most of his days napping in sunbeams and demanding to be hand-fed gourmet salmon treats? It was like calling a marshmallow dangerous.

The absurdity of the situation hit the master and his shoulders began to shake with barely suppressed laughter. And Binx, still tucked securely under his arm, had the audacity to start purring contentedly, as if he hadn't just caused a small war in the middle of our morning walk.

The bulldog owner, sensing perhaps that he was fighting a losing battle against the rising tide of hilarity, gathered what was left of his dignity (and his still-bewildered pet) and stormed off down the path, muttering darkly about reporting us to the local authorities.

As we watched him go, the master finally allowed his laughter to break free, a rich, full-bodied sound that seemed to chase away the last of the morning's tension.

"Oh, Binx," he chuckled, scratching the unrepentant feline behind the ears. "What are we going to do with you, you impossible creature?"

Binx, for his part, simply yawned and settled more comfortably into the master's arms, the very picture of feline innocence.

And as for me? Well, I couldn't help but feel a newfound respect for my feline housemate. He might be a pain in the tail most days, but there was no denying he had a flair for the dramatic. And in a world that too often felt mundane and predictable, wasn't that something to be celebrated?

And really, what more could any dog (or cat, or human) ask for?

A Final Farewell to a Feisty Friend

It was a day I had been dreading, a day that came far too soon after we had already said goodbye to our dear friend George. Ludwig, the feisty bearded dragon who had once ruled our household with an iron claw, had grown old and weak. His passing, though not unexpected, left a gaping hole in our hearts.

I lay near Ludwig's tank, my head heavy with grief. It seemed like only yesterday that George had left us, succumbing to the illness that had plagued him for so long. The mistress had been devastated, her eyes red-rimmed and her voice hoarse from crying.

And now, here we were again, gathered around Ludwig's tank as he took his final breaths.

The mistress sat beside the tank, her hand resting on the glass. "Oh, Ludwig," she whispered, her voice cracking. "You were such a fighter, right until the end. Thank you for bringing so much joy and laughter into our lives."

Ludwig's eyes fluttered open, and for a moment, I swore I saw a flicker of his old spirit in their depths. He let out a soft huff, his beard twitching ever so slightly.

I inched closer, my heart heavy. "Ludwig, my friend," I said softly. "I know we had our differences, but I always admired your spunk. You made life interesting, that's for sure. George may have left us too soon, but I know he's waiting for you on the other side."

My feline pack, too, seemed to sense the gravity of the moment. They approached the tank, their heads bowed in respect. Even though they had once been the target of Ludwig's relentless pursuit, each seemed to mourn his passing.

And then, with a final shuddering breath, Ludwig was gone. The mistress let out a quiet sob, her shoulders shaking as she cradled his tiny body in her hands.

I felt a deep, aching sadness wash over me. First George, and now Ludwig—two friends, so different in personality yet both so deeply loved, taken from us far too soon. It seemed almost cruel, the way life could give and take away so quickly.

Over the next few days, the house was filled with a quiet sorrow. The absence of George's gentle presence and Ludwig's fiery spirit was keenly felt by all of us. The mistress tried her best to keep our spirits up, offering extra treats and cuddles, but even she seemed lost in her grief.

As I lay in my bed at night, I couldn't help but think of all the times Ludwig had chased the kitties around the house, his little legs pumping furiously as he'd pursued them with single-minded determination. I thought of the way he would puff out his beard and strut around like he owned the place, never backing down from a challenge.

And I thought of George, sweet gentle George, who had been the yin to Ludwig's yang. The two of them had been an unlikely pair, but they had brought so much joy and laughter into our lives.

Slowly but surely, life began to go on.

And me? I did my best to be there for everyone, offering a comforting paw or a gentle nuzzle whenever I sensed they needed it. Because that's what family does—we support each other through the good times and the bad, through the laughter and the tears.

Ludwig and George may have been small in stature, but they left an enormous impact on our lives. They taught us about the power of resilience, the importance of living life to the fullest, and the unbreakable bonds of love that can form between the most unlikely of friends.

And though they are gone, they will never be forgotten. Their spirits will live on in our hearts and in the stories we tell, a reminder to cherish every moment we have with the ones we love.

Rest easy, my scaly friends, until we meet again on the other side, where the crickets are plentiful, and the basking spots are always warm. You may be gone from this world, but you will never be gone from our hearts. Farewell, Ludwig and George. You were loved more than you could ever know.

Princely Pampering at the Poochie Palace

"Who's ready for a lil' spruce up?" The mistress called out in a singsong tone from the hallway. I immediately perked up from my cosy nest of blankets, tail dusting the floor in anticipatory thumps.

Aha, it must have been that time again—my standing primping appointment at the palace of poochie pampering! I bound out to greet her, spinning in a circle and letting out a few rumbling "woofs" of unbridled excitement.

The mistress chuckled indulgently and ruffled the scruff around my neck. "That's what I thought! You always know when it's grooming day, don't you, handsome?"

She gave me an appraising sniff and puckered grimace. "And not a moment too soon by the smell of things, phew! Let's get you looking—and smelling—like the royalty you are, Benny Boo."

A few enthusiastic licks to her cheek and I was happily toddling along towards the car, visions of suds and brushes dancing in my head.

You see, while I do so relish getting perpetually grubby from rollicking outdoors, even a strapping pup like me has an appreciation for the finer grooming arts. There's just something so indulgently resetting about a good fluff 'n' buff every month or so—a recharge and refurb of my ruddy dignity!

As we pulled into the familiar parking lot of Gorgeous Grooming For Good Dogs, my tail achievement levels kicked into overdrive. I was doing that funny butt wiggle I could never quite control, drunk on the ambrosial scents of perfumed shampoos and pork dog treats that always seemed to be wafting through these hallowed halls.

The human receptionists lavished me with gushing greetings, scratching beneath my chin from every angle. One even snuck me a tiny turkey schmacko while surreptitiously checking my appointment time.

"Fancy a puppuccino while you wait, Ben?" she stage whispered, as if I didn't already know the script by heart.

I bark out an enthusiastic "woof!" in response, performing a few giddy spins on my haunches for good measure. Like they even needed to ask—half the reason I got so stoked for these appointments was the prospect of that heavenly snack guaranteed to kick things off.

For the uninitiated, a puppuccino is essentially a tiny cup of whipped cream topped with a delicate dog biscuit. But to discriminating gourmands such as myself, it's an ambrosia of the highest order—cool, velvety decadence one rollick away from terribly uncouth licking. I made appreciative snuffles over each luscious spoonful as my humans awaited my grooming turn.

At last, the call came for me to be whisked behind those magical stainless steel gates and into the inner sanctum. The smiling human ushered me towards a raised grooming tub, then . . . the indignities began! Off came the collar, leaving me in my inglorious nude-fur state.

Don't look so aghast—even we canine elite require a deep cleansing purge and evacuation every so often. And honestly, I'd come to appreciate how thoroughly these skilled groomers went about depolluting and destinking me.

First came the full soaking rinse and vigorous scrubbing with industrial dehairing solution strong enough to clear out even the most stubborn sheddings and grime wedgings. Don't ask me what's in it besides unicorn dandruff or whatever; I just know that by the time the massaging is done my once downy coat flows sleeker than an eel.

Then it was on to the more . . . intimate areas in need of, let's say, excavating. The various nooks and craggy recesses that sand and forest detritus tend to become so enthusiastically compounded in over time. No furry fold was left un-vacuumed, I'll put it that way!

Admittedly, this phase did tend to leave my dignity in shreds as I was expertly Hoovered from stern to stem. You could practically hear the groomer's internal monologue of "Good lord, how does he not just combust from grime buildup?" as she unearthed leavings and detritus of weeks past.

But no complaints from me! As uncomfortable as it might have felt in the moment, the end result of rebirth and rejuvenation was more than worth the fleeting indignities. By the time I was standing there sleek and glistening and pulsing with fresh-scented shampoo tingle, I felt practically reincarnated.

They always insisted on fully styling me too, going the whole nine slobbery yards with shears and bristle brushing to accentuate the flowing contours of my princely physique—even resorting to a rather undignified canine-sized blow dryer to fluff me up into an impressive Fabiolus of sorts. Eat your heart out, Binkster!

Personally, I think I rocked the shaggier Insouciant Poet vibe better, but I let them enjoy their craft without comment.

Finally, to the grooming grand finale—the breath freshener! A few spritzes of that godawful but thankfully momentary stinging freshener mist did indeed leave my chops tasting like a lawn ornament. But hey, nobody's perfect. At least now the mistress wouldn't get sinus clearance from planting affectionate licks to her cheek.

In the end though, the true pièce de resistance were always those irresistible accessories and send-off treats! Would it be a smart bandana this month or another stylish nautical necktie? Personally, I voted for the dapper-as-hell fedora and walking stick combo, but nobody ever asked me.

No matter what finery got bestowed upon my newly glorified self, the groomer would always make a point of leading us past those tantalising snack bars one final time. And this time, oho, this time I was utterly powerless to resist the smorgasbord of gourmet confits and biscuits on proud display.

As if I'd been half-starved for months, I went to town scarfing up every tidbit left on offer—a gourmet swirl of chicken-bacon-cheddar here, a puppucake drizzled with beefy frosting there. The usual parade of slobbery mortification for the mistress as I worked my way around the sample trays, entirely ignoring her pleas for restraint and decorum.

By the time we were striding proudly homeward though, I felt like the most gloriously replenished hound in doggy kingdom—handsome and debonair with my new neckwear, a pronounced jaunt in my step from all the carbo loading. But most importantly, an inner glow of absolved soul and scrubbed good hygiene.

As the mistress was so fond of proclaiming whenever we completed these cathartic renewal cycles: "There's my good boy! Don't you feel like a fresh new young pup again?"

Why yes, yes I did! Like all the grubby, smelly, scruffy indignities of the past month had been buffed and blown into oblivion. Another grand rotation around the Sun achieved, and many more deliriously romping adventures to come!

Best start rolling around in some fresh dirt immediately . . .

A Tale of Jealousy and a Monkey's Demise

It all started with a stuffed monkey. A silly little thing, with big googly eyes and a perpetual grin stitched onto its face. But to Binx, that monkey was everything. And to me, well, it was the bane of my existence.

You see, Binx had a special relationship with that monkey. He would carry it around in his mouth, kneading it with his paws and, um, humping it with great enthusiasm. At first, I was perplexed by this behaviour. But then the mistress explained that it was a normal thing for male cats to do. Something about hormones and instincts, I suppose.

"It's perfectly natural, Ben," she said, scratching behind my ears. "Binx is just doing what comes naturally to him."

But that didn't make it any easier to watch. Every time Binx started going at it with that monkey, I felt a twinge of jealousy. Why didn't he ever want to play with me like that? Was I not good enough?

One day, while Binx was out on one of his usual jaunts around the neighbourhood, I found myself alone with the monkey. It sat there, mocking me with its stupid grin. Something inside me snapped.

Before I knew what was happening, I had the monkey in my jaws, shaking it back and forth like a ragdoll. The seams split, and stuffing flew everywhere, covering the garden in a layer of white fluff.

"Take that, you homewrecking primate!" I growled, my tail wagging with savage satisfaction.

By the time I was done, the monkey was nothing more than a pile of rags. I felt a momentary pang of guilt, but it was quickly overshadowed by a sense of triumph. Binx would have to find a new plaything now.

Later that day, the master came out to tidy up the garden and mow the lawn. He scooped up the remains of the monkey, muttering something about "damn birds making a mess," and tossed it in the bin without a second thought.

I watched from the window, my tail thumping happily. Mission accomplished.

But my victory was short-lived. Without his beloved monkey, Binx turned his attentions to the mistress's tartan blanket. And her dressing gown. And pretty much any soft, fluffy thing he could get his paws on.

The mistress was not amused. "Binx, stop that!" she scolded, trying to shoo him away from her blanket. "What's gotten into you?"

I watched from my bed, trying to suppress a chuckle. It seemed that Binx's hormones were still raging, monkey or no monkey.

As the days went by, Binx's antics only escalated. He would drag the mistress's clothes out of the laundry basket, leaving a trail of socks and underwear in his wake. He even tried to hump the mistress's dressing gown...whilst she was still in it!

"We need to do something about this," the mistress said, exasperated. "He's driving me crazy!"

I couldn't help but feel a little guilty. After all, it was my fault that Binx's monkey had met its untimely demise. But what could I do? It's not like I could have gone out and bought him a new one.

And so, life went on in our household. Binx continued to hump anything and everything he could get his paws on, much to the mistress's chagrin. And I continued to watch from the sidelines, feeling a strange mix of amusement and guilt.

But despite the chaos and the destroyed blankets, there was still plenty of love and laughter to go around.

In the end, I realised that maybe I didn't need to be jealous of Binx's monkey after all. Because even without it, he was still the same lovable, mischievous cat he had always been. And I was still the loyal, faithful dog who would always be there for my family, no matter what.

So what if Binx liked to hump blankets and dressing gowns? That was just part of who he was. And if we had each other, everything would be just fine.

Even if it meant occasionally finding a sock in my water bowl or a discarded tartan blanket on the living room floor. Because that's just life with a cat like Binx. And I wouldn't have it any other way.

A Picture-Perfect Moment (Almost)

As an old dog who's seen his fair share of family milestones, I've learned to recognise the telltale signs of an Important Event brewing. There's a certain electricity in the air, a flurry of activity that sets my tail wagging with anticipation. And on this summer afternoon, our little household was positively buzzing with excitement.

Our Bronwyn, no longer the gangly pup I once knew but a young woman on the cusp of adulthood, was preparing for her school prom. I'd watched from my favourite sunspot in the living room as she'd flitted about, a whirlwind of perfume and sparkly fabric, her face alight with a mixture of nerves and excitement.

"Oh, Ben," she'd sighed, pausing in her preparations to give me a scratch behind the ears. "Can you believe it? Your girl's all grown up."

I'd responded with a gentle woof, trying to convey that no matter how tall she grew or how fancy her dress, she'd always be my girl—the one who'd snuck me treats under the table and curled up with me during thunderstorms.

As the appointed hour drew near, the entire family gathered at the front of the house for the traditional pre-prom photoshoot. The master, armed with his fancy camera and a determined glint in his eye, was directing operations with all the gravity of a military commander.

"Right then, Bron, just stand over there. Perfect! Now, give us a smile. That's it!"

I watched from my spot on the patio, my head cocked to one side as I tried to make sense of all the fuss. Humans and their rituals, I tell you. Always a source of bewilderment for a simple hound like myself.

But then, as the master fiddled with his camera settings, I felt a familiar pressure in my bladder. Now, ordinarily, I'm a good boy who knows to do his business in the designated spots. But something about the charged atmosphere, the nervous energy radiating off my humans, must have short-circuited my usual decorum.

Before I knew quite what I was doing, I found myself trotting into the frame, right as the master was about to take the perfect shot.

"Ben, no!" I heard him cry, but it was too late. Nature was calling, and who was I to argue?

There I was, in all my canine glory, photobombing Bronwyn's prom pictures and cheerfully relieving myself. The look on the master's face was a sight to behold - a comical mix of horror, exasperation, and reluctant amusement.

Bronwyn, bless her heart, collapsed into a fit of giggles, her carefully applied makeup in danger of running as tears of laughter streamed down her face.

"Oh, Ben," she gasped between peals of laughter. "Trust you to make this moment unforgettable!"

The mistress, ever the voice of reason, managed to keep a straight face for all of three seconds before joining in the laughter. "Well," she chuckled, wiping tears from her eyes, "I suppose this is one for the family album. 'Bronwyn's prom, featuring Ben's impromptu performance.'"

As for me, well, I'd finished my business and was feeling quite pleased with myself. I'd contributed to the occasion in my own unique way, hadn't I? Tail wagging, I trotted back to my humans, ready to accept their praise for my starring role in the photoshoot.

The master, having recovered from his initial shock, shook his head ruefully. "You old rascal," he said, giving me a reluctant pat. "I suppose we should have known you'd want to be part of the action."

Once the laughter had subsided and I'd been gently shooed back indoors, the photoshoot resumed. But there was a lightness to the proceedings now, the earlier tension dissolved by my impromptu performance.

Bronwyn's smile was brighter, more natural, as she posed for the camera. The master and mistress exchanged fond glances, their eyes twinkling with shared mirth. And I, well, I basked in the warmth of my family's laughter, content in the knowledge that I'd played my part in making this milestone truly memorable.

As I watched Bronwyn twirl in her sapphire blue gown, ready to embark on this new adventure, I felt a swell of pride and a twinge of nostalgia. My little girl, all grown up. But in that moment, with the echo of laughter still hanging in the air and the memory of her unrestrained giggles fresh in my mind, I knew that no matter how old she got, no matter how far she roamed, a part of her would always be that little girl who found joy in the simple, silly moments.

And really, isn't that what life's all about? Finding laughter in the unexpected, joy in the imperfect, and love in the everyday chaos of family life. As I settled back into my spot, watching my humans bustle about with their preparations, I couldn't help but feel that I'd done my job as the family dog rather well.

After all, years from now, when Bronwyn looks back on her prom night, I'd wager it won't be the perfect pose or the immaculate hair she remembers most fondly. No, it'll be the moment her old dog Ben decided to make his mark on the occasion—quite literally—and turned a formal photoshoot into a moment of pure, unbridled family joy.

And if that's not a job well done for a loyal old hound, well, I don't know what is.

GENTLE BEN

Lip Smackin' Good

It started off innocuously enough, as most deeply ingrained doggy habits tend to do. A little lip smacking here, an occasional bout of noisy slurping there—all part and parcel of being a canine connoisseur ever savouring life's simple flavours.

For the master and kids, my episodes of open-mouthed indulgence were generally met with the usual repertoire of long-suffering eye rolls and half-hearted scolding. But I'm a dog—such primitive pleasures are hardwired into my very being. Like asking a fish not to swim or a bird to forgo aviation. Impossible.

No, it wasn't until the mistress's . . . condition . . . arose that my innocent penchant for lip smacking transcended mere eccentricity into a full-blown four-legged plague upon the household. You see, some months back, the mistress had come down with a rather curious affliction having to do with her ears.

The medical name was a tongue-twisting mouthful even I could scarcely pronounce—recruited idiopathic sensory modality dysphoria or some such nonsense. In layman's terms, it meant her hearing had become extremely sensitised, especially to high-pitched sounds in a certain frequency range.

As you might imagine, the constant smacking of canine lips fell straight into that unpleasant audio sweet spot. What was little more than white noise to the rest of the family caused the mistress's nerves to become exquisitely frayed whenever I began working my slobbery magic.

It started innocently enough. I'd be lounging across the room as the mistress tried to relax with her nightly shows. Suddenly, the telltale smacking would commence, my jowls flapping with wild abandon as I lapped up the residual deliciousness coating my chops.

"Ben, kindly stop that incessant lip licking before I go completely starkers," she'd plead through gritted teeth, hands pressed firmly over her ears.

I'd glance up, ears cocked in feigned guilelessness despite my mouth continuing to work away with even more exaggerated vigour. Hey, if she was going to mention it...

"Niall, won't you do something about that infernal racket?" she'd beseech the master. Then, voice edged with desperation: "He's going to drive me right round the bend, I swear it!"

The master, ever the devoted partner, would dutifully intervene with the usual commands to cease and desist my maddening oral shenanigans. I'd manage perhaps thirty seconds before the compulsive licking resumed in earnest, now accompanied by exaggerated gasps of pleasure with each imaginary flavour explosion.

It wasn't that I was intentionally trying to torment the poor woman, not at first. We dogs simply can't resist answering the impassioned call of our inner Pavlovian pup, that unquenchable drive to lick and smack and revel in the vividly visceral experiences our tastebuds were designed to deliver.

Any dog owner worth their weight in Gravy-Bones could tell you, excessive lip smacking is often a big flashing neon sign broadcasting a dogged attempt to command their human's undivided attention.

Boredom, excitement, anxiousness . . . you name the emotional trigger, and obsessive licking is typically Fido's default response. It's an ingrained remnant of our puppy salad days, when we'd lick our mothers' faces to instigate feeding and affection in equal measure.

Nowadays, that hardwired reflex tends to get a mite misdirected toward our human companions in a form of endearingly desperate plea: "Hey hooman, can't you see how interesting and adorable I'm being over here? A little rub behind the ears wouldn't go amiss, friend!"

Of course, my own licking proclivities soon took on a more . . . calculated bent once I cottoned onto just how triggering the sounds were for the mistress's condition. You could call it petty mischief-making of a dog desperate for his daily dose of novelty and human engagement.

I'd wait until she was settled in to read, then strategically position myself in her line of sight before letting the smacking and slurping commence. Like a perverted circus geek revelling in his sideshow talents, I'd put on an entire performance of it, licking myself from chest fur to tail-tip as noisily as my slobbery jowls could muster.

The mistress's escalating reactions ran the gamut from silent rage to apoplectic meltdowns. One minute she'd be reaching for the remote to crank the volume past shriek-inducing levels. The next, she'd be hightailing it out of the room altogether with a book to escape my torturous serenade in the blessed silence of another part of the house.

"I swear Niall, one more hour listening to that ungodly racket and I may just take a sledgehammer to my own eardrums!" she proclaimed one particularly bothersome afternoon.

I cocked an ear, mischievous gaze sliding her way only to find she'd already burrowed herself beneath a protective mound of pillows and blankets. All that was visible was a small cavern for situating her painfully sensitive ears, sealed off against further assault by my endlessly enthusiastic lapping.

The master looked from huddled pile to dog and back again, features oscillating between fond exasperation and restrained panic. I could practically see the wheels turning as he calculated how best to defuse this rapidly escalating domestic powder keg before the mistress well and truly combusted.

"Alright boy, up you get," he addressed me in a hushed tone, gesturing for me to follow.

My ears pricked with intrigue and the promise of treats galore. A very long walkies with countless coveted snacks and belly rubs aplenty once I'd well and thoroughly tuckered myself out in a glorious flurry of "chase me" was clearly on the cards.

Practically levitating off the floor with glee, I trotted obediently after the master, pausing only to bestow one final lick of faux-contrition upon the blanketed grump-lump that was my mistress.

As the door swung shut behind us, I caught a glimpse of her smiling wearily back at me from beneath the covers. For all her blustering about my biohazardous licking, we both knew she wouldn't have had it any other way. This was all just part of the delightfully dysfunctional dynamic keeping our family unit afloat.

The master and I indulged in some quality one-on-one bonding.

And if that involved a little therapeutic licking along the way, all the better to wring a few extra treats and ear scratches out of the experience. Like mother, like son: the urge to partake of life's simple tactile pleasures was a hardwired imperative we sophisticates of the canine persuasion couldn't easily shake. I called it my birthright, my way of reminding the family that at my core, I'd always be a simple pup at heart. And maybe, just maybe, helping the mistress retain her sense of humour along the way amidst her debilitating aural affliction.

The Wanderer's Return

Look, I'm a loyal dog through and through, but even I must admit there's something undeniably cool about a street-smart cat. Binx, that sleek black prowler who roamed our neighbourhood, was the epitome of feline mystique.

During the day, you'd find him lounging in prime sunbathing spots, sprawled across the top of the backyard fence or curled up on the porch steps like a furry solar panel. But as soon as night fell, Binx transformed into a stealthy predator. His eyes glowed like little LEDs as he patrolled his self-proclaimed territory.

The backyard became his personal kingdom, and woe betide any stray cat who dared to challenge his reign. It was like watching a tiny, furry bouncer keeping unwanted guests out of an exclusive nightclub.

Our evening walks were when Binx and I really connected. It was like we had this unspoken bromance going on. While my human and I took a leisurely stroll, stopping to sniff every interesting smell (because let's face it, that's half the fun of walks), Binx would slink along parallel to us. He moved like a tiny ninja, weaving between trees and fences as if he was on some covert ops mission.

I bet we looked like a weird duo to anyone watching—the overeager, goofy dog and his mysterious feline sidekick. But we had this whole yin and yang thing going on, you know? Two different species vibing on the same wavelength.

I tried to play it cool, pretending not to notice how Binx tensed up whenever I got too close to his invisible boundaries. And Binx, being the chill cat he was, gave me my space too. It was like we had this unwritten agreement: "You do you, I'll do me, and we'll both pretend the other isn't totally fascinating."

That was our dynamic—me, the social butterfly making friends with every human and lamppost in sight, and Binx, the aloof observer who probably thought he was too cool for school. Classic dog and cat, am I right?

But then, one summer night, everything went sideways. One minute Binx was there, doing his usual ghostly cat routine, and the next—poof! Vanished like he'd been beamed up by some feline-specific UFO.

Cue three weeks of intense "Lost Cat" drama. My humans went into full detective mode, plastering the neighbourhood with "Missing" posters and blowing up every local Facebook group with Binx's photos. We took marathon walks, sniffing every bush and alley for any trace of our AWOL kitty.

I left my "pee-mail" everywhere, hoping Binx would pick up on my scent and follow it home. "Yo, furball! If you can smell this, you're getting warmer!"

The kids eventually gave up and went back to their TikTok and video games, but my master and mistress were relentless. They drove around at night with the windows down, calling Binx's name like they were auditioning for a very niche version of "The Voice."

We got a few false alarms from well-meaning neighbours. "I saw a black cat!" Yeah, turns out there's more than one black cat in the world. Who knew?

You could practically see my humans' hope fading with each dead end. It was like watching someone's phone battery slowly die when there's no charger in sight.

Then, just when we were about to throw in the towel, my mistress's phone pinged. Some random person had spotted a cat that might be Binx! Talk about an emotional rollercoaster.

Long story short, Binx eventually showed up on our doorstep looking like he'd been through the kitty version of a hardcore music festival. Scrawny, scruffy, but alive.

The reunion was like something out of a cheesy rom-com—tears, hugs, and enough fur flying to stuff a small pillow. I hung back, letting my pack have their moment. My job as Binx's unofficial search party was done.

Over the next few weeks, Binx bounced back like a champ. With enough premium cat food and sneaky table scraps, he was back to his sleek, majestic self in no time. But something had changed. It was like he'd gone through some kind of feline epiphany during his walkabout.

No more wild nights out for this kitty. Binx became more of a homebody, sticking closer to the house during his nightly patrols. It was like he'd traded in his party animal lifestyle for a more chill, Netflix-and-catnip vibe.

We never figured out where Binx had been or what had happened to him. Some mysteries are meant to stay mysteries, I guess. Maybe he'd joined a secret cat cult or gone on a vision quest. Who knows?

GENTLE BEN

But here's the thing—it didn't really matter. What mattered was that our weird little family was whole again. Dog, cat, humans—we were all back together, appreciating each other a little more after the scare.

So now, Binx and I are back to our old routine. Nighttime patrols, silent companionship, the occasional shared look that says, "Can you believe these humans?" We're the neighbourhood watch team nobody asked for but everybody needs.

Because at the end of the day, home isn't just a place. It's a feeling. It's knowing you've got a pack (or pride, in Binx's case) that has your back. And whether you're a dog person or a cat person, that's something we can all get behind.

So bring on the night and all its mysteries. Binx and I are ready for whatever comes our way. Just two cool dudes, living our best lives, one walk at a time.

A New Pack in Pandemic Times

Just when I thought I had our little family unit all figured out, life threw us a series of curveballs that would change everything. It all started when Jacob came home one day, his face lit up with a glow I hadn't seen in years. By his side was a lovely young woman named Caitlin, and holding her hand was the most adorable little human I'd ever laid eyes on—Mia.

From the moment they walked through the door, I knew our pack was about to change in the most wonderful way. Mia's eyes widened with excitement when she saw me, and I couldn't help but wag my tail in response. There's something about the unbridled joy of a child that even an old dog like me can't resist.

"Doggy!" Mia squealed, looking up at her mum for permission.

Caitlin smiled warmly. "That's Ben, sweetie. Why don't you say hello?"

I sat patiently, my tail thumping against the floor as Mia cautiously approached. Her tiny hand reached out, and I gently nuzzled it, earning a delighted giggle that seemed to light up the whole room.

Little did we know that this chance meeting would turn into something much more significant. Not long after, the first whispers of a strange new illness began filtering into our cosy family bubble. The mistress and master huddled around the telly each evening, murmuring worriedly about some sort of novel coronavirus making its way across distant borders.

At first, it all seemed rather abstract and far removed from our day-to-day routines. The occasional news clips of overcrowded hospitals and masked humans scurrying through empty streets felt more like dispatches from an alternate reality than harbingers of an imminent threat.

But then, with an almost eerie synchronicity, the sinister tendrils of the pandemic began snaking their way into every corner of our once-predictable existence. It started with the little things—the master frantically scouring store shelves for hand sanitizer and loo roll.

Before we knew it, the entire rhythm of our household had been upended by the lockdown orders sweeping the nation. When the pandemic hit and lockdown was announced, Jacob invited Caitlin and Mia to stay with us. Our cosy home suddenly became a lot livelier, and I couldn't have been happier about it.

At first, I must confess a certain shameful thrill at having my humans all to myself 24/7. With nowhere to go and no one to see, surely they'd have ample time to lavish me with belly rubs and games of fetch! But as the days bled into weeks and the weeks into months, the novelty of our new normal quickly wore thin.

The master, though still dutifully logging his hours and collecting his usual salary from the home office, grew increasingly morose as the endless Zoom meetings and isolation began to take their toll. He'd spend hours listlessly clicking through news sites, his brow furrowed and jaw clenched as he absorbed the latest tallies of infections and economic devastation.

"Christ, love, have you seen this?" he'd mutter to the mistress, jabbing a finger at some ominous graph or tweet. "They're saying we could be in for a second wave come autumn. At this rate, who knows how long it'll be before we can see anyone in person again..."

The mistress did her best to maintain a cheery front, but even she couldn't fully mask the weariness and worry nibbling away at her usually indomitable spirit.

As for yours truly, I did my best to provide what cold comfort I could, my doggy heart aching in tandem with my humans' unspoken fears. I made it my mission to be there for every stress-baking marathon and gloomy news binge, my head resting on a knee or my tail thumping out a steady rhythm of reassurance.

As the weeks turned into months, Caitlin and Mia became an integral part of our household. Their presence seemed to fill a void I hadn't even realised was there. The house was fuller, noisier, and infinitely more joyful, even as we all struggled with the confines of lockdown.

Mia quickly became my constant companion. She had an energy that matched my own in my younger years, and I found myself rediscovering the joys of playfulness that I thought I'd left behind. We'd spend hours in the garden playing fetch (although I'll admit, sometimes I was more interested in the belly rubs than returning the ball).

I made sure to be extra gentle with Mia, always mindful of my size compared to her tiny frame. When she'd stumble during our play sessions, I'd be right there, offering my sturdy body for her to lean on as she regained her balance.

As the lockdown continued, our days fell into a new routine of enjoying whatever small adventures we could find within the confines of our home and garden.

Through it all, I did my best to cling to the few certainties still tethering me to some semblance of stability. The feel of the mistress's fingers scratching that secret sweet spot behind my ears, or the sound of the master's off-key whistling as he paced endless laps around the living room.

But more than anything, it was the moments of hard-won levity, the slivers of light puncturing an otherwise unrelenting stretch of darkness, that kept me moored and mindful. The board game night that devolved into helpless belly laughs instead. The first tentative picnic in the park once restrictions began to ease, the sheer bliss of sun-warmed grass and the happy shrieks of reunited friends almost enough to blot out the ever-present thrum of anxiety.

And then, finally, came that glorious day when the first vaccines began rolling out, a scientific marvel delivered to beat back the invisible beast holding us all hostage. As vaccination rates climbed and infection rates dropped, the government slowly began to ease lockdown restrictions.

It was like a collective sigh of relief swept through our household. The mistress, always one for finding silver linings, decided to use this newfound freedom to explore local attractions that were now reopening.

One of our first trips was to see the 'iron dinosaurs' at a nearby sculpture park. Mia rode on the master's shoulders, pointing excitedly at each metal beast we encountered. I trotted alongside, my nose working overtime to catalogue all the new and exciting scents. The way Mia's eyes lit up at each new discovery reminded me of the simple joys in life that we often forget as we grow older.

Our trips to the seaside were another highlight. I watched in amusement as she danced at the edge of the waves, squealing every time the cold water touched her toes. I, of course, stayed close by, ever the vigilant protector.

These outings felt like a rebirth, a rediscovery of the world beyond our four walls. The sun on our faces, the wind in our fur (or hair), the sheer joy of movement and exploration—it was intoxicating. Even the master and mistress seemed lighter, their smiles coming more easily as we ventured out into this post-lockdown world.

Caitlin and Mia continued to stay with us. I overheard Jacob and the mistress talking about them possibly moving in permanently until they could afford a home of their own, and I couldn't have been more thrilled. The thought of Mia's laughter and Caitlin's gentle presence becoming a permanent fixture in our home filled me with a warmth that rivalled the cosiest sunbeam.

Looking back, I realise that this unexpected turn of events was exactly what our family needed. In a time of global uncertainty and fear, we found joy, love, and a renewed sense of purpose. Mia's innocent wonder at the world reminded us all to appreciate the little things, while Caitlin's strength and kindness in the face of adversity inspired us to be better.

As I watched my humans cling to each other, their laughter mingling with muffled sobs of catharsis, I felt my own doggy heart swell with fierce, unshakable pride. We may have been battered and bone-weary, our nerves frayed and our patience tested to the limit . . . but, we were still standing. Still together, still fighting, still finding small everyday miracles amidst a world gone mad.

As for me, well, I may be getting on in years, but Mia's presence has sparked a new vitality in this old dog. Every day brings new adventures, new games, and new opportunities to protect and love this expanded pack of mine.

Who knew that during a global pandemic, our family would grow in the most beautiful and unexpected way? Life, as I've learned, has a funny way of bringing us exactly what we need, exactly when we need it. And as I curl up each night, with Mia's gentle pat on my head, I know that our pack is complete, our bonds stronger than ever.

And really, what more could a loyal hound ask for? In the end, the true essence of pack is being there for each other through thick and thin—through boring and blitz.

Whatever challenges the future may bring, I'm ready to face them—with my expanded family by my side, and the sound of Mia's laughter to light the way. One day at a time, one cuddle at a time, one adventure at a time . . . that's the ticket. We've weathered the storm of this pandemic together, and now, as we step back into the world, our little family unit is stronger than ever.

A Terrifying Twist in Our COVID Tale

After months of hunkering down in our cosy quarantine bubble, the world finally began to cautiously reopen. Shops dusted off their shelves, pubs fired up their grills, and workers tentatively returned to their respective jobsites—all with a host of new safety measures in place.

For Bronwyn, this meant a long-awaited return to her job at the local McDonald's. She'd been back at work for a week, diligently masking up and sanitising her hands raw after every customer interaction. The mistress, bless her perpetually fretting heart, had fussed and clucked over her like a mother hen each morning as she'd headed out the door.

"You're being extra careful, aren't you, love?" she'd ask.

Bronwyn, to her credit, bore her mum's hovering with good-natured patience. "Yes, Mum," she'd sigh, pressing a quick kiss to the mistress's cheek before ducking out the door. "I promise not to take any unnecessary risks."

If only we'd known then just how quickly that promise would be put to the test.

It started with a slight tickle in the back of Bronwyn's throat one evening after her shift—nothing major, just a niggling irritation that had her clearing it a bit more frequently than usual. By the next morning, that tickle had blossomed into a full-blown cough—deep, hacking spasms that left her gasping for air and sent icy tendrils of dread unfurling in the pit of my stomach.

The mistress, her brow furrowed with worry, reached out to feel Bronwyn's forehead. "You're warm, love," she murmured, her own voice tight with barely concealed fear. "I think it's best if you stay home from work today and get tested. Just to be on the safe side."

Bronwyn opened her mouth as if to protest, but one look at the naked concern on her mum's face seemed to change her mind. "Alright," she agreed, shoulders slumping in defeat. "I'll call my manager and let her know."

By the time Bronwyn had completed the home test and the results came back, the heavy sense of foreboding that had settled over the house felt almost palpable.

"It's positive," Bronwyn confirmed. "I have COVID."

From that moment on, our once-bustling home transformed into a tightly controlled isolation ward. Bronwyn returning to bed and sleeping most of her ill days away, until she finally felt like her normal self once more. As for yours truly, I did what I could to provide emotional support and companionship from a safe distance.

But it was only a matter of time before the mistress's overtaxed system began to buckle. It started with a cough—a dry, hacking thing that seemed to rattle her from the inside out. At first, she tried to play it off, but the cough deepened and intensified, leaving her breathless. When a spasm of coughing overtook her, so violent and prolonged that it left her gasping for air, the master dialled 111. When the mistress struggled to speak to the human on the other line the phone was passed back to the master. His face paled and he moved with a speed I had never witnessed before out of the front door. He arrived less than ten minutes later with a box in his hands. I . . . well, I simply sat in the middle of the chaos, my old doggy heart clenched in fear as I watched my beloved family navigate this terrifying new crisis.

The paramedics arrived within minutes of the master's return, their faces grim but determined beneath their protective gear. They queried why 111 had sent the master for a defibrillator and reassured the mistress—who had panic in her eyes—that it was not needed. They examined the mistress and monitored her with different devices. The lead paramedic, a kind-faced woman with serious eyes, crouched down to the mistress's level. "Kirsty," she said gently, "with your underlying health conditions we feel that the hospital is not the best place for you right now, and we would rather you stay at home and try to manage your symptoms here. But I need you to understand that if your condition deteriorates any further, we won't have a choice but to admit you. This virus is nothing to take lightly."

The mistress closed her eyes for a long moment, tears leaking from beneath her lashes. "I understand," she managed between coughing bouts.

The paramedic turned to the master. "Go to the chemist and pick up a blood oxygen monitor to keep an eye on her oxygen levels. If they drop any further or she gets any worse, call 999." They left with those strict instructions.

The master sagged against the wall in relief, scrubbing a hand over his haggard face as he watched them go. And then it was just us again—a family clinging together during the storm, battered but unbroken. I watched the mistress closely whilst the master returned the defibrillator and followed the paramedic's instructions.

Over the next few days, the master and I tag-teamed our efforts to care for the mistress. He'd monitor her vitals and temperature with an obsessive eye. I'd curl up at her feet on the occasions that she managed to move from the bedroom to the living room.

The mistress, though still frightfully weak, gradually started to regain her appetite, though she was still prone to long naps and shortness of breath. The master, his face lined with a weariness no amount of sleep could fully erase, began to allow himself the occasional smile and chuckle.

Bronwyn returned to work, her mask and hand sanitiser now permanent fixtures in her daily routine. And I . . . well, I did what I'd always done. I loved my family, fiercely and unconditionally. I stood guard over them as they slept, ready to sound the alarm at the first hint of distress. I nuzzled away their tears and coaxed out their laughter and reminded them, in my own small way, that no matter how dark the road ahead might seem . . . we would walk it together.

As the mistress was fond of saying, "This too shall pass." And though the journey had been unspeakably hard and the scars would linger long after the virus itself had retreated . . . I knew in my bones that she was right.

We were battered, but unbroken. Weary, but unbowed. And most importantly, we were together—a family forged in the crucible of crisis, our bond stronger than any disease could hope to sever.

And so, as the world outside continued to grapple with the unimaginable, we clung to the one thing that had always seen us through the storms of life: love. Messy, imperfect, hard-won love . . . but love all the same.

For in the end, it was the only thing that mattered. The only thing that would endure, long after the worst had passed. And as I curled up at the foot of the mistress's bed each night, listening to the steady rise and fall of her breathing and the soft snores of my beloved family . . . I knew I was exactly where I needed to be.

Come what may, we would face it as we always had—together. And somehow, some way . . . we would emerge on the other side, stronger and more grateful than ever for the simple, precious gift of being alive.

A Feline Frenzy

Life had just begun to settle into a new post-lockdown rhythm when Jacob and Caitlin decided to shake things up in the most delightful way possible: by bringing home a pair of fuzzy little bundles of mischief.

Enter Simba and Millie, two wide-eyed balls of fluff who instantly stole the hearts of everyone in the household (yes, even a grizzled old dog like me couldn't resist their charms).

Simba came first, a tiny tabby with an outsized personality that belied his diminutive stature. From the moment he arrived, he made it clear that he was not content to be a mere pet—oh, no. This kitten had designs on ruling the roost.

"Isn't she just precious?" Jacob cooed, cradling the mewling scrap of fur in his arms as he introduced us.

The mistress, ever the font of feline wisdom, took one look at the kitten's nether regions and chuckled. "I hate to break it to you, love," she said gently, "but I think you'll find that's a 'he,' not a 'she.' Looks like little Simba here is a master of disguise!"

Jacob's face flushed as red as Simba's tiny nose, but he quickly recovered with a sheepish grin. "Oops," he laughed, scratching the kitten behind the ears. "Guess we'll have to adjust our pronouns accordingly. Welcome home, little man."

Millie arrived a day later, a ginger tabby with an impish gleam in her eye that immediately set my tail wagging. She and Simba took to each other like catnip to a scratching post, tumbling and tussling across every inch of the house in a whirlwind of mischief.

The arrival of the kittens was a bittersweet joy. While we delighted in their antics and the way they brought fresh laughter and lightness to the household, we couldn't help but feel a pang of nostalgia for our own dearly departed feline friends.

"They remind me so much of May and Suki," Bronwyn sighed one evening, watching Simba and Millie chase each other's tails in dizzying circles. "It's like having a little piece of them back, you know?"

I nuzzled her hand in silent agreement, my own heart aching with remembrance. But as the days turned to weeks and the kittens began to grow and thrive, I found myself marvelling at the way they seamlessly wove themselves into the fabric of our family.

Simba seemed to have a special bond with the mistress. From the very beginning, he gravitated towards her like a moon in orbit, constantly seeking out her lap or shoulders as his preferred perch.

"Well, would you look at that," the master chuckled one afternoon as Simba curled himself around the mistress's neck like a purring scarf. "Looks like someone's found his person."

The mistress, her eyes soft with affection, stroked Simba's glossy fur and smiled. "I've heard that cats often choose their own humans," she mused. "Something about pheromones and compatibility. I guess Simba just knows a kindred spirit when he meets one."

And indeed, the connection between woman and kitten only seemed to grow stronger with each passing day. Wherever the mistress went, Simba was sure to follow—a constant shadow of devotion and companionship.

Even I had to admit, it was a beautiful thing to witness. After all the mistress had endured with her health challenges and the toll of the pandemic, seeing her face light up with pure, uncomplicated joy every time Simba nuzzled her cheek or purred in her ear . . . well, it was enough to make even a crusty old dog's heart grow three sizes.

But of course, the course of true love (feline or otherwise) never did run smooth. And as Simba and Millie grew from playful kittens to frisky young adults, it became increasingly clear that their bond ran deeper than simple sibling affection.

"Oh my god," Caitlin gasped one morning, as she walked in on the two cats engaged in a passionate embrace. "Are they . . .? Please tell me they're not actually . . ."

But the mistress, ever the realist, simply shook her head and sighed. "I'm afraid they are, love. Looks like we'll be having a little feline shotgun wedding on our hands soon enough."

And sure enough, a few short months later, Millie was round as a beach ball and mewling piteously as she waddled around the house in search of the perfect nesting spot.

When the blessed event finally arrived, it was all hands on deck as the family gathered around to welcome the newest members of our unorthodox little clan. Four perfect miniatures of their parents, all downy fur and tiny pink noses and ears that seemed far too large for their wee heads.

"Would you look at that," Jacob marvelled, cradling one of the ginger boys in his hands. "A little ginger snap, just like his mummy."

"And this little girl," Caitlin cooed, stroking the smallest kitten's silky back. "I think we should call her Rosie."

But even amidst the flurry of naming and nosing and general newborn adoration, it was clear that Simba only had eyes for one person: the mistress.

As she sat cross-legged on the floor, Simba curled himself around her protectively. His rumbling purr seemed to vibrate through the very floorboards, a tangible expression of his deep bond with the woman who had become his whole world.

"I hope you know you're not getting rid of him now," the master teased Jacob and Caitlin. "That cat has well and truly claimed my wife as his own. I'm just the hired help at this point."

Jacob and Caitlin exchanged a knowing glance, their eyes soft with understanding. "We kind of figured as much," Jacob admitted. "Simba's always been more her cat than ours, if we're being honest. It only seems right that he stays with her."

The mistress, her eyes brimming with tears of gratitude, gathered Simba into her arms and buried her face in his fur. "Thank you," she whispered, her voice muffled but thick with emotion. "I promise I'll love him enough for all of us."

And so it was decided. When the time came for Jacob and Caitlin to move into their own place a few months later, Simba stayed behind with the mistress. Millie went with them, along with little Rosie and the two ginger boys (who had been adopted out to loving families of their own).

But the mistress couldn't bear to part with all her grand-kittens. And so little Nala, the spitting image of her father right down to the tiny white patch on her chest, became a permanent fixture in our household as well.

As for me, I found myself once again marvelling at the strange and wonderful twists of fate that had brought us all together. Simba and Nala, Millie and her kittens, Jacob and Caitlin and Bronwyn and the master and mistress . . . we were a motley crew, to be sure. A patchwork quilt of a family, stitched together by love and circumstance and the odd bit of catnip.

A Bittersweet Transition

Life, I've come to realise, is a series of hellos and goodbyes. A constant ebb and flow of beginnings and endings, arrivals and departures, each one shaping us in ways both big and small.

And so it was that our little family found ourselves amid yet another bittersweet transition, as young Jacob prepared to spread his wings and fly the proverbial coop.

It wasn't a decision he had come to lightly, I knew. Jacob had always been a homebody at heart, content to orbit within the warm and familiar gravity of the family unit. But love, as it so often does, had a way of shifting even the most steadfast of trajectories.

And Caitlin? She was Jacob's true north, the guiding star by which he charted his course. Where she went, he would follow—even if that meant venturing far beyond the cosy confines of our little corner of the world.

"It's time, Mum," he said softly one evening, as the family gathered around the dinner table to absorb the news. "Caitlin and Mia . . . they're my future. We've decided to live in Newcastle. It's best for Mia, as her dad doesn't drive."

The mistress, her eyes bright with unshed tears, reached out to clasp her son's hand in a fierce grip. "I understand," she whispered, her voice thick with emotion. "But that doesn't make it any easier to bear."

The master, ever the stoic optimist, simply clapped Jacob on the shoulder and offered a watery smile. "You're doing the right thing, son. Following your heart, even when it leads you down an unfamiliar path. That's all any parent can ever hope for their child."

Watching the scene unfold from my spot curled up under the table, I felt my own doggy heart constrict with a complex tangle of emotions. Pride, for the brave and beautiful young man Jacob had grown into. Sadness, for the impending loss of his steady presence in our daily lives. And joy, bittersweet but genuine, for the exciting new chapter he was about to embark upon.

Because if there was one thing I had learned over the course of my long and eventful life, it was that change, painful as it may be, was also essential for growth. And as much as I would miss Jacob's gentle scratches behind the ears . . . I knew that this was the natural order of things. The way it was meant to be.

And so, with heavy hearts but hopeful spirits, we helped Jacob pack up his life into a jumble of boxes and bags. We reminisced over old photos and inside jokes, marvelling at the way time seemed to flow like quicksilver when you weren't paying attention.

We made grand plans for visits, determined not to let the miles between us strain the bonds that had always held us together. And when the day finally came for Jacob to load up his car and hit the road, bound for Newcastle . . . we hugged and laughed and cried and hugged some more, until it felt like our hearts might burst from the sheer overwhelming weight of it all.

"Don't be a stranger, yeah?" the mistress sniffled, cupping Jacob's face between her palms.

Jacob, his voice thick with emotion, could only nod and pull his mum in for one last fierce embrace. "We'll be back for visits before you even have a chance to miss us."

With a final round of watery smiles and lingering hugs, he was gone—off to chase his dreams and build a beautiful life with the little family he had created. And just like that, the rhythm of our household shifted once again into a new and unfamiliar cadence.

At first, the absence of Jacob's energy was a palpable thing—a Jacob-shaped hole in the very fabric of our daily existence.

But as the days turned into weeks and the weeks into months, we gradually settled into our new normal. Bronwyn and Jay, who had taken to spending more and more time at our place in the wake of Jacob's departure, became an even more integral part of the family fabric.

With their easy laughter and playful banter, they brought a much-needed breath of fresh air into the house. Bronwyn, who had always been the more social butterfly of the two siblings, took it upon herself to organise regular game nights and movie marathons, determined to keep us all from falling into a rut of melancholy.

"Just because Jacob's gone doesn't mean we stop living, too," she declared firmly, brandishing a bowl of popcorn and a stack of DVDs. "We're still a family, even if we're a bit more spread out now. And families stick together, no matter what."

Jay, who had been steadily winning over the hearts of the master and mistress with his quiet dependability and fierce devotion to Bronwyn, simply nodded in agreement. "Absolutely. You're stuck with us now, whether you like it or not."

And stuck with them we were—in the very best way possible. Slowly but surely, the rhythms of our days began to feel familiar again, even in their newness.

As for me, I found great solace in the quieter moments—the peaceful early mornings when it was just me and my thoughts, the long walks in the park with the master by my side, the lazy afternoons curled up in a patch of sunlight.

It wasn't that I didn't miss the bustle and energy of a full house—I did, desperately at times. But there was also something to be said for the gentle lulls, the spaces in between where we could simply breathe and be still and appreciate all that we had.

Because that was the thing about family, I was coming to realise. It was always changing, always growing, always shifting into new and beautiful configurations. But at its core, it remained the same—a tapestry woven from the threads of love and laughter, tears and triumphs, hellos and goodbyes.

And as I watched my little pack navigate this latest twist in our shared journey, I couldn't help but feel a swell of pride and gratitude for all that we had weathered together. The joys and the sorrows, the gains and the losses . . . they had all shaped us into the beautifully imperfect, perfectly resilient clan we were today.

So here's to you, Jacob, as you embark on this new and exciting chapter. May your days be filled with love and laughter, and may you always carry a little piece of home wherever you go.

And to the rest of us, holding down the fort in your absence? We'll be here, keeping the fires burning bright and the kettle always on for a cuppa. Ready to welcome you back with wagging tails and open arms, whenever your heart leads you home again.

Because that's the beauty of family, isn't it? No matter how far we roam or how much we grow, we always have a soft place to land. A constant in a world of variables, a touchstone to remind us of who we are and where we came from.

And as I curled up at the mistress's feet, listening to the gentle murmur of conversation and the clink of tea mugs in the kitchen, I knew that I was exactly where I was meant to be.

Home, with my pack. Weathering the storms and savouring the sweet spots, one day at a time. And really, what more could a lucky old dog like me ask for?

Absolutely nothing. Absolutely everything. And all the precious moments in between.

The Puppy Invasion

Just when I thought our household had reached its maximum capacity for four-legged mischief, the universe decided to throw in the form of two pint-sized bundles of energy and enthusiasm.

Enter Coco and Cookie, the Springer Cocker puppies that Jacob and Caitlin had recently welcomed into their growing family. With their silky ears, soulful eyes, and perpetually wagging tails, they were the very picture of canine cuteness.

But as I would soon learn, looks can be deceiving. And these two pups? They were trouble with a capital T.

It all started when Jacob and Caitlin announced they were taking a much-needed holiday, their first real getaway since the pandemic had turned all our lives upside down. They were hesitant to leave their furry charges behind, still being so young and in need of constant supervision.

"I hate to even ask," Jacob fretted. "But would you and Dad be willing to watch Coco and Cookie for a few days? I know it's a lot to take on, but we really need this break and the pups are still too young for a kennel and I just don't know what else to do, and—"

The mistress, bless her perpetually generous heart, simply waved away his concerns with a smile. "Of course we'll watch them, love. You two deserve a chance to recharge. And besides, how much trouble could two little puppies possibly be?"

Oh, the naivety. The sheer, unbridled optimism. If only we had known then what we were getting ourselves into.

From the moment those two whirling dervishes bounded through the front door, our once-peaceful home descended into absolute chaos. They were everywhere at once, a blur of wagging tails and clicking claws and high-pitched yips of excitement.

My feline companions, who had grown accustomed to a certain level of decorum and respectability in their golden years, took one look at the furry interlopers and promptly disappeared into the highest hidey-holes they could find. Even I, a seasoned old dog who had weathered my fair share of canine antics over the years, found myself feeling a bit overwhelmed by the sheer energy radiating off those pups.

"Cookie! Coco! No jumping on the furniture!" the mistress called out, frantically trying to corral the bouncing balls of fluff as they ricocheted off the couch and armchairs like furry pinballs. "Sit! Stay! Oh, for heaven's sake..."

But the pups, bless their overexcited little hearts, were too far gone in the throes of puppy glee to pay her any mind. They tumbled and tussled, nipping at each other's ears and chasing their tails in dizzying circles until they finally collapsed in a panting heap of tangled limbs and lolling tongues.

"Well," the master remarked wryly, surveying the destruction left in their wake. "I think it's safe to say we're in for an interesting few days."

And oh, how right he was. Over the next 72 hours, our home became a veritable obstacle course of chewed-up shoes and shredded pillows and suspicious puddles that seemed to materialise out of thin air. The master and mistress, who had initially been so confident in their ability to wrangle the rambunctious pups, quickly realised they were in over their heads.

"I don't understand," the mistress panted, dragging a squirming Cookie away from the toilet paper roll she had just gleefully unspooled across the entire upstairs hallway. "I've raised puppies before. I know how to train them. But these two...it's like they have a never-ending supply of energy!"

The master, who had just finished mopping up yet another "accident" on the kitchen floor, could only shake his head in commiseration. "I think it's a Springer Spaniel thing," he said. "I've heard they're notorious for being high-energy and mischievous, especially when they're young. They need a lot of exercise and mental stimulation to keep them out of trouble."

And so, in a valiant effort to burn off some of that excess puppy zeal, the master and Jay took to walking Coco and Cookie separately. Jay would take one, the master the other, in hopes that the individual attention would help them focus and behave.

But even that proved to be a challenge. Because as soon as one pup started to settle into a good walking rhythm, the other would inevitably do something to set them off again. A squirrel darting across the path, a leaf skittering by on the breeze . . . it was all fair game for a full-blown puppy freakout.

"Coco, no! Leave it!" the master would shout, struggling to keep the wiggling puppy from lunging after every passing distraction. "Heel! Heel, I say!"

But Coco, bless his eager little heart, was too busy trying to befriend every rock and stick and blade of grass to pay any attention to silly things like commands. And Cookie, who seemed to delight in nothing more than winding up her brother until he was a quivering mess of excitement, would simply sit back and watch the chaos unfold with a satisfied little smirk on her furry face.

As for me, I found myself torn between exasperation and begrudging amusement at the puppy antics unfolding around me. On the one hand, it was exhausting trying to maintain any semblance of dignity or decorum with those two little tornadoes tearing through the house at all hours. But on the other hand . . . well, there was just something so endearing about their unbridled joy and zest for life.

Even when Coco, in a misguided attempt to emulate his new hero (that would be yours truly), took to following me around like a shadow and mimicking my every move. I would plod into the kitchen for a drink of water, and there he would be, tripping over his own oversized paws in his haste to keep up. I would flop down for a nap in my favourite sunbeam, and he would immediately curl up right next to me, his little puppy snores tickling my ear.

It was equal parts adorable and annoying, if I'm being honest. But I couldn't really hold it against the little guy. After all, he was just doing what puppies do best—exploring the world with boundless curiosity and enthusiasm, and latching onto anything (or anyone) that caught his fancy.

And even Cookie, for all her mischief-making ways, had her moments of sweetness. Like when she would finally wear herself out after a particularly rambunctious play session and crawl into the mistress's lap with a contented little sigh. The mistress would stroke her silky ears and murmur soft endearments, and for a moment, all would be calm and right in the world.

But alas, such moments of tranquillity were all too fleeting amid the puppy pandemonium. And by the time Jacob and Caitlin returned from their trip, the master and mistress were well and truly ready to hand the reins back over to the pups' rightful owners.

"Oh, my babies!" Caitlin cooed, scooping up a wriggling Coco and Cookie and showering them with kisses. "Were you good for Nana and Grandad?"

The master and mistress exchanged a wordless glance, a whole unspoken conversation passing between them in the space of a heartbeat.

"They were . . . spirited," the mistress said diplomatically, her smile a touch strained around the edges. "But we survived. Somehow."

Jacob, bless him, had the good grace to look sheepish as he surveyed the damage left in the pups' wake. "We can't thank you enough for watching them," he said, rubbing the back of his neck. "I know they can be a handful. We're working on their training, but it's a process."

And work on it they did, with the diligence and patience of the saints they surely were. Over the next few months, Jacob and Caitlin poured their hearts and souls into moulding Coco and Cookie into the best versions of themselves. They hired trainers and watched endless online tutorials, practicing commands and positive reinforcement techniques until the pups started to show glimmers of the good dogs they could be.

But even with all their efforts, it became increasingly clear that the demands of raising two high-energy puppies were more than they could manage on top of their already hectic lives. Jacob was putting in long hours at his new job, and Caitlin had her hands full caring for an increasingly active Mia.

It was a heartbreaking realisation for them, the acknowledgement that as much as they loved Coco and Cookie, they simply couldn't give them the time and attention they needed to thrive. And so, with heavy hearts and no small amount of tears, they made the difficult decision to rehome the pups.

"It's not fair to them," Caitlin sniffled. "They deserve so much more than we can give them right now."

The mistress, her own eyes misty, murmured words of comfort and reassurance. "You're doing the right thing, love. The brave thing. Those pups are going to have a wonderful life with their new family, and it's all because you loved them enough to let them go."

I couldn't help but feel a pang of bittersweet affection for the little scamps. They may have turned our world upside down for a few wild and woolly days, but they had also brought a fresh burst of energy and laughter into our lives when we needed it most.

And isn't that just the way of it with dogs? We come into your lives like furry little wrecking balls, all boundless enthusiasm and unconditional love. We test your patience and challenge your sanity, but we also remind you of the simple joys in life—the thrill of a good belly rub, the comfort of a warm body curled up next to yours at the end of a long day.

We may not be perfect (though some of us come pretty darn close, if I do say so myself), but we love with every fibre of our being. And in the end, that's really all that matters.

So here's to you, Coco and Cookie. May your new lives be filled with endless Tennis balls and belly rubs and all the squirrels you can chase. And may you always remember the family that loved you first, even if they couldn't be the ones to see you through to the end.

Because that's the thing about love—it doesn't always look the way we think it should. Sometimes, the greatest act of love is knowing when to let go, trusting that the story will continue without you in ways you never could have imagined.

And as for me? Well, I may be an old dog, but I'd like to think I've still got a few tricks up my sleeve. Like knowing when to lend a comforting paw or a sympathetic ear, even (especially) to the creatures who drive me the craziest.

Because at the end of the day, we're all just stumbling through this big old world the best we can. And if we can do it with a wagging tail and an open heart . . . well, that's not a bad way to go through life, if you ask me.

Slowing Down

These old bones just aren't what they used to be. Nowadays it takes me a few groans and stretches to heave myself up off my bed. My back legs don't have the same spring in them—in fact, sometimes they almost seem to give out from under me entirely!

"Easy does it, Benny boy," the mistress will coo, steadying me with a gentle hand. Her face crinkles up with concern whenever I take a wobbly step. I can read her thoughts plain as day: her puppy is getting on in years.

It's true, I'm slowing down nowadays. But I like to think I'm aging with a certain dignified grace. A few achy joints and a greying muzzle haven't dampened my spirits one bit! I may move a little slower, but I'm still the same loyal, loving lug I've always been.

Although . . . I do have to admit, climbing up and down stairs has become a bit of an ordeal. My back legs just don't have the strength anymore, especially first thing after a good night's sleep. It's almost comical watching me tentatively tackle that first step, then pause for a breather before summoning the courage for the next one. Halfway up, I'm already panting like I've just run a marathon!

The mistress recognised my difficulties quickly. One day, she and the master lugged their big comfy bed down to the living room and set it up alongside mine. No more stairs to navigate at all!

"How's that, hmm?" the mistress said, giving me a wink. "Now we can be downstairs buddies together."

Ah, that's right—in her older ages, the mistress has mobility troubles of her own. We're quite the pair, stumbling and shuffling around together! At least I know I've got good company on my level.

To be honest, I do miss being able to bound up to the kids' bedrooms like I used to. Some of my fondest memories are of keeping night vigils beside their beds as pups. I'd sleep close enough that I could hear their drowsy snuffles and sleep-murmurs. Standing guard over their dreams, ready to chase any monsters away with a protective woof.

On nights when they had bad dreams, they'd reach down to clutch my fur for comfort until they fell back into peaceful slumber. Those were such special bonding moments between us. I knew they always felt safest having their canine pal curled up loyally by their side.

Nowanights, I must make do with curling up outside the mistress's bedroom door downstairs. The hard laminate floors in there are too unforgiving for my aging bones and joints. But I appreciate being close by all the same, listening to the gentle sounds of her and the master's breathing while I stand watch.

My body may be slowing down, but my spirit is just as lively as ever. I'm still constantly wagging and prancing around, doing happy spins to greet my family each morning. The mistress laughs at my "saying good morning to my creaky old self" routine—I can't help but dance a little jig while I get my back legs aligned and stretched out for the day ahead!

She calls me her "senior sweetheart" now and showers me with all the gentle ear scratches and brushing that us elderly pups need. And I'm MORE than happy to accept all the pampering, You've earned this comfort in your twilight days, she always reminds me. I can't really argue with that logic!

So while I may not be able to romp and play with the same puppy vigour I once had, we're making the most of my golden years together. I'll keep shuffling along at my own pace, stopping to sniff each rose along the way. And my family will be right there at my side as we go, loving me no matter how slow and creaky I become.

These days, I like to tell myself I'm not slowing down. I'm simply . . . appreciating the sweetness of life's smallest details while they still last. One contented snore, belly rub, and "good boy" at a time.

The Mailman's Magic Touch

Okay, so these old bones of mine might creak like a rusty gate, but catch a whiff of that familiar scent wafting through the mail slot? It's like someone hit the reset button on my arthritis!

I heave myself up from my memory foam dog bed, back legs wobbling like I'm auditioning for a canine remake of "Bambi on Ice." The mistress materialises at my side faster than you can say "senior dog supplement."

"Easy there, Ben," she fusses, her face a map of worry lines. I can practically hear her thinking, "When did my puppy turn into a furry grandpa?"

But I flash her my patented doggy grin, tongue lolling out like I'm trying to catch invisible treats. Sure, I might be rocking the silver fox look these days, but inside? Still the same goofball she's always loved.

The doorbell chimes, and suddenly I'm vibrating like a phone on silent mode. My ears perk up, catching that unmistakable scent of parcels and… wait for it… treats! My tail goes into overdrive, making my back end look like I'm trying to twerk (badly).

The mistress lets me wobble past as she opens the door. She knows the drill—our friendly neighbourhood mail carrier is basically Santa Claus in a polyester uniform.

And there he is, our jolly postman, looking like he's about to burst out of his official blues. He gives me a wink that says, "You know what time it is, buddy," and starts digging in his pocket like he's searching for the meaning of life.

The smell hits me like a wave of pure doggy ecstasy. Chicken jerky treats! I'm already doing my happy dance, which these days looks less like dancing and more like I'm having a very enthusiastic seizure.

"Hold your horses, ya old rascal!" Joe (that's our postman) teases, holding the treats just out of reach. "Let's see those world-famous tricks first, eh?"

Challenge accepted! I let out a bark that's part battle cry, part asthma attack, and launch into my greatest hits. Picture a geriatric dog trying to recreate a viral TikTok dance challenge, and you're pretty much there. It's not pretty, but it gets the job done.

Joe howls with laughter like I've just told the world's funniest joke. "You've still got it, you maniac! A true showman to the end." The treats rain down like manna from heaven, and I'm on them faster than you can say "senior diet kibble."

I make a big show of enjoying each morsel, complete with dramatic chomps and contented old-man grumbles. Joe watches with that "kids these days" kind of amusement, even though we've been doing this song and dance for years.

"Whoa there, speed racer," he chuckles, steadying me as I nearly face-plant in my eagerness. "Don't want you throwing out your back over a bit of jerky!"

I give him my best "who, me?" look. We both know I'm not as spry as I used to be, but that doesn't mean I can't still appreciate life's simple pleasures, right?

"Actually," Joe says, suddenly looking like he's about to pitch us a set of steak knives, "I've got a business proposition for you folks."

The mistress and master exchange a look that says, "This ought to be good."

"I've been taking classes, see, in this thing called Animal Reiki," he explains, puffing up with pride. "It's like... imagine if your dog could get a spa day for his soul."

I'm already half-asleep at the mention of "spa day." Sign me up, coach!

"All Ben needs to do is chill out for about 30 minutes while I use my healing hands to get his doggy chi flowing right," Joe continues, warming to his topic. "It's like acupuncture, but without the needles and with 100% more belly rubs."

I have no clue what he's on about, but if it means I get to nap while someone pets me? I'm all in.

As if to demonstrate, Joe reaches over and gives me an ear scratch that nearly makes my leg kick involuntarily. I melt into a puddle of geriatric bliss.

"See that?" he grins triumphantly. "He's already reaching doggy nirvana! How about we schedule a session for next Sunday? I'll bring the healing vibes, you provide the tea and biscuits."

With one last conspiratorial wink at me, he's off, whistling a jaunty tune. Meanwhile, I'm drifting off into la-la land, dreaming of cosmic walkies and infinite treat dispensers.

I mean, seriously, what more could an old timer like me ask for? Treats for my tummy AND a spiritual tune-up delivered right to my door? That's the kind of serendipity that keeps my tail wagging, even when my joints say, "no more!"

From that day on, every knock at the door sets my tail wagging with Pavlovian excitement. No matter how stiff I might be feeling, I always make the effort to hobble over and give our visitors a good sniff-down. You never know who might be hiding treats in their pockets, right?

Besides, I've perfected the art of the "pitiful old dog" look. One well-timed whimper, and even the most hard-hearted visitor turns into a treat-dispensing machine. It's a tough job, but somebody's got to do it.

So yeah, I might be getting a bit long in the tooth, and my coat might be more salt than pepper these days. But my enthusiasm for life's simple joys? That's still firing on all cylinders.

So bring on the magical mailmen, the surprise snacks, and the weird new-age pet therapies. This old dog is ready for whatever treats – edible or spiritual – the universe wants to throw my way. After all, who says you can't teach an old dog new tricks? Especially if those tricks come with biscuits!

The Void Where Companionship Used to Be

Life, as I've come to learn over my many years as a faithful family dog, is an ever-shifting kaleidoscope of change and adaptation. Just when you think you've settled into a comfortable routine, the universe has a way of shaking things up and rearranging the pieces into a whole new pattern.

For our little household, that change came in the form of a bold new venture that had been percolating in the mistress's mind ever since the thrilling but tumultuous release of her first self-published book back in November 2019.

You see, while the experience of bringing her words to life and sharing them with the world had been immensely fulfilling, it had also illuminated the myriad challenges and pitfalls that come with navigating the daunting world of independent publishing.

From formatting errors and distribution snafus to the sheer overwhelm of trying to market and promote the book on her own, the mistress had found herself wishing time and again for a supportive community of fellow authors and publishing professionals to lean on.

And so, with the same determination and creative verve, the mistress set about bringing her vision to life. She would create a one-stop shop for self-published authors—a cosy haven where they could find the resources, guidance, and camaraderie they needed to bring their literary dreams to fruition.

She called it The Book Dragon, a nod to both her own fiery passion for the written word and the mythical beasts of lore known for guarding treasure troves of knowledge and wisdom.

Bronwyn, ever the supportive daughter and tech-savvy sidekick, immediately volunteered to help bring the concept to life. With barely a second thought, she handed in her notice at McDonald's and threw herself into the whirlwind of planning and preparation alongside the mistress.

"This is going to be amazing, Mum," she gushed, her eyes sparkling with the same fierce determination that had seen her through countless late-night study sessions and early morning shifts. "We're going to create something really special here—a true haven for writers and readers alike."

The mistress, her own face aglow with the thrill of a new creative challenge, could only nod in agreement. "I couldn't do this without you, love," she said, pulling Bronwyn in for a fierce hug. "You've always been my rock, my sounding board, my partner in crime. Having you by my side in this venture means the world to me."

And so, with the help of a veritable village of loved ones—from the mistress's father and stepmother to the master's own doting mum, not to mention Jay's seemingly endless well of good-natured support—The Book Dragon slowly began to take shape.

They found a satisfactory location, painted the walls in soothing shades of green and gold, hung twinkling fairy lights and cozy reading nooks, and filled the shelves with an eclectic mix of self-published gems just waiting to be discovered.

And on July 4th, 2022, after months of hard work and countless cups of tea fuelling late-night planning sessions, The Book Dragon officially opened its doors to the world.

It was a joyous occasion, filled with laughter and tears and the buzzing energy of a community coming together to celebrate something truly special. Authors mingled with readers, swapping stories and signing books and forging connections that would last long after the last page was turned.

The mistress, resplendent in a flowing dress the colour of a perfect summer sky, flitted from conversation to conversation with the grace and ease of a true hostess. Her smile, so often shadowed by the weight of chronic pain and fatigue, shone bright and unencumbered—a testament to the healing power of purpose and passion.

And Bronwyn, the unsung hero of the operation, worked tirelessly behind the scenes to ensure that every detail was attended to with care and precision. From managing the mistress's complex medical needs to troubleshooting last-minute tech hiccups, she proved herself to be the true heart and soul of The Book Dragon.

But amidst the whirlwind of activity and excitement, there was one member of the family who found himself struggling to adjust to this new normal. And that, I'm afraid, was yours truly.

You see, with the mistress and Bronwyn now spending most of their waking hours at the shop, and the master and Jay off at their own respective workplaces, I suddenly found myself facing long stretches of solitude that I had never quite experienced before.

Oh, sure, I had the cats to keep me company—but as any self-respecting dog will tell you, felines are hardly a substitute for the warm, reassuring presence of one's human pack. They were content to while away the hours napping in sunbeams and chasing errant dust motes, blissfully unconcerned with the growing sense of unease that had begun to gnaw at my belly.

At first, I tried to rationalise the feeling away. After all, I was no stranger to the occasional bout of alone time. I had long since learned to amuse myself with a well-worn chew toy or a leisurely patrol of the perimeter while the family attended to their daily obligations.

But as the days stretched into weeks and the absences grew longer and more frequent, I found myself slipping into a state of near-constant anxiety. Every creak of the floorboards, every rustle of the wind through the trees, sent my heart racing and my nerves jangling with the irrational fear that something terrible had happened to my beloved humans.

I paced the halls in agitated circles, my nose pressed to the ground in a vain attempt to catch some lingering trace of the mistress's perfume or the master's woodsy aftershave. I whined and whimpered by the front door, my tail drooping and my ears flat against my skull as the minutes ticked by with agonising slowness.

Even when the family did finally return home each evening, weary but elated from another successful day at The Book Dragon, I found little comfort in their presence. I was too wound up, too on edge, to fully relax into the usual rituals of belly rubs and ear scratches.

It wasn't until the mistress, ever the astute observer, noticed the telltale signs of my distress that the pieces finally clicked into place.

"Oh, Ben," she murmured, sinking to her knees and gathering me into her arms. "I think you might be experiencing separation anxiety, old boy. I'm so sorry we didn't realise sooner."

The term was unfamiliar to me, but the symptoms she went on to describe—the pacing, the whining, the inability to settle even in the presence of my loved ones—sounded all too painfully accurate.

The mistress, her brow furrowed with concern, immediately set about researching strategies to help alleviate my distress. She read articles and consulted with our trusted veterinarian, determined to find a way to help me feel safe and secure even during so much change.

And slowly but surely, with the help of a few key adjustments and a whole lot of patience and love, I began to find my footing once again.

They started leaving me with familiar items imbued with their scent—a well-worn t-shirt, a favourite blanket—to provide a tangible reminder of their presence even when they were physically absent. They invested in puzzle toys and interactive feeders to keep my mind engaged and my body busy during the long stretches of solitude.

And perhaps most importantly, they made a point of carving out dedicated chunks of quality time each day to shower me with the affection and attention I so desperately craved. Long walks in the park, lazy cuddles, impromptu games of fetch in the garden—these small but meaningful gestures went a long way towards filling the void that their absence had left behind.

It wasn't always easy, and there were still moments when the old anxiety would rear its ugly head and send me into a tailspin of nervous energy. But with each passing day, I found myself growing a little bit stronger, a little bit more resilient in the face of change.

And through it all, I had the unwavering love and support of my family to lean on. They might not have been physically present every minute of every day, but I knew deep in my bones that I was never truly alone.

Their hearts were with me always, a steadfast anchor in the choppy seas of uncertainty. And that knowledge, more than any fancy toy or comforting scent, was what ultimately helped me weather the storm of separation anxiety.

Because at the end of the day, that's what family is all about—being there for each other through thick and thin, even (especially) when the going gets tough. It's about adapting and evolving together, finding new ways to connect and support one another as the world around us shifts and changes.

And as I watched the mistress and Bronwyn pour their hearts into The Book Dragon, creating a welcoming haven for kindred spirits and fellow dreamers, I couldn't help but feel a swell of pride and gratitude for the incredible pack I belonged to.

They might not have had all the answers, and they certainly weren't perfect by any stretch of the imagination. But they loved fiercely, and they loved well. And in a world that can so often feel cold and chaotic, that kind of love is a rare and precious gift.

GENTLE BEN

So here's to the ups and downs, the triumphs and the challenges, the hellos and the goodbyes that make up the messy, beautiful tapestry of family life. Here's to the comfort of routine and the thrill of new adventures, the solace of solitude and the joy of coming together after time apart.

And most of all, here's to the unbreakable bonds of love and loyalty that see us through it all—the ties that bind us, even as the world around us ebbs and flows like the tide.

As long as I have my pack by my side and a warm place to rest my head at the end of the day, I know that everything will be alright in the end. Because that's the magic of family—it makes even the hardest of times feel just a little bit easier, a little bit brighter, a little bit more bearable.

And for a lucky old dog like me, that's more than enough to chase away the darkest of shadows and fill even the emptiest of spaces with light and love and the unshakable certainty of belonging.

My Girl's All Grown Up

I could sense something big was happening. There was an excited energy pulsing through the house. Bronwyn was rushing around collecting boxes and babbling on about "setting up the new place" while Jay loaded up his car.

Ah, that's what it was—my girl was finally leaving the nest!

I trailed along behind Bronwyn as she dashed from room to room, watching her carefully wrap up her belongings. Posters and photos came off the walls, drawers were emptied, shelves stripped bare. With each item packed away, another little piece of her childhood slipped into the past.

In the kitchen, the mistress was trying to keep a brave face but I could see her eyes getting misty behind her smile. My old tail gave an empathetic thump against the floor. My Bronwyn had blossomed and it was time to spread her wings. As much as I'd miss having her around, I felt immensely proud watching her take this big scary leap into the future.

Soon enough, the car was loaded up and good-byes were being said. Bronwyn swept me up into her arms for one last lingering cuddle.

"Who's gonna keep me out of trouble now, eh boy?" she whispered, scratching behind my ears. "I'm gonna miss you so much."

I licked her cheek, telling her the same without words. She would be just fine out there. My job was done—I'd watched over her all these years and now it was time for her next adventure. Whatever challenges life sent her way, I knew her spirit was ready.

With a final wave, Bronwyn hopped into the car and they were off, driving towards their exciting new chapter. A lump formed in my throat as I watched them go. But I was mostly filled with pride and a warm happiness that she was forging her own path at last.

Bronwyn had finally grown up. But she'll always be my little girl.

Empty Nest, Full Heart

The house had a stillness to it these days that made my ear tufts twitch. No more thundering footsteps up and down the halls, no squabbles over the TV remote, no one raiding the fridge every five minutes. Just . . . quiet.

At first, I rather enjoyed the peace and tranquillity. I could lounge undisturbed in my favourite sunny spot or take an epic snooze. No little human hands grabbing at me or loud music drowning out my snores. Bliss!

But then I noticed a shift in the mistress. The bounce in her step was gone, replaced by a sort of flatness. She started spending long periods just staring off into space, sad crinkles around her eyes. Sometimes I'd catch her standing in Bronwyn's old bedroom, fingertips grazing over the bare shelves and surfaces as if she could still sense her daughter's spirit lingering there.

"They've all grown up and moved on now," she would say quietly, more to herself than me. "Just you and me rattling around in this big old place, Ben."

That's when the howling would start. Mournful, unsettling howls that made my hackles prickle with concern. The master tried to console her, pulling her into a warm embrace and murmuring soothing words. But I could see the crestfallen look in his eyes too. Their baby birds had left the nest.

One evening, I nuzzled open the door to find the mistress huddled on the sofa, puffy tears streaking down her cheeks

"Oh Benny Boo," she sobbed, using my sweet nickname from when I was a puppy. "I'm so lonely without them! How am I supposed to get used to this empty nest syndrome?"

Aha, so that's what the master called it! This "empty nest" thing must have been causing the mistress's sadness now that Bronwyn and Jay were out living their lives. I couldn't imagine how hard it must feel to have your babies grow up and leave you behind. No wonder she felt so lost.

Slinking closer, I rested my chin on her knee with my most adoring "pleeease don't cry" expression. The mistress sniffled, scratching behind my ears in that way she knew calmed me down.

"You're a good boy, you know that?" she mumbled, using her free hand to ruffle my fur. "Always here for me, even when the house feels so big and quiet."

I leaned into her touch, soaking up every ounce of comfort she had to give. If anybody could ease this empty nest syndrome, it was me.

For a while we just lay there, my head resting on her lap while she stroked me meditatively. A few more tears rolled down her cheeks but she seemed . . . comforted.

Over the next few weeks, I made it my dog duty to lavish the mistress with companionship and affection.

Slowly but surely, her smiles became more frequent and her howls faded away. The mistress was adjusting to her new normal—just her, the master, me, and my cat friends keeping her company.

Some days she would even joke about it, "Well Ben, I may be an empty nester but at least I've still got my fur babies to look after!"

I knew she still missed Bronwyn, Jacob and Adam terribly at times. But I was always there with a furry cuddle and a loyal listening ear to ease the ache. Whether it was chasing away night terrors or entertaining with silly tricks, I gave her a million little reasons to smile and laugh again.

Because that's the wonderful gift we dogs can provide—unconditional love, gentle companionship, and a life brimming with simple joys. We can't make the empty nest feeling disappear entirely, but we sure can fill the space with so much warmth and affection that it doesn't feel so empty anymore.

With me by her side, the mistress realised she didn't need to fear the quiet—it was simply the turning of a page into an exciting new chapter. And I would happily write the next pages alongside her, our paw prints marking the way together.

The Return of the Black Dog

Things had been off lately in our little pack. The mistress seemed . . . dimmer somehow. Like a candle flickering in the depths instead of burning bright. Her smiles didn't quite reach her eyes and the spark was missing from her usual cheery greetings.

"Good morning, my old mutt," she'd mumble as she shuffled into the kitchen each day, mechanically preparing her tea. The way she said it sounded almost like an apology rather than an affectionate nickname.

The whole energy of the house had shifted into something heavy and melancholic. Rooms that once buzzed with laughter and activity now gathered dust in stifling silence. Even the master's booming footsteps seemed muffled, like he was walking through a dense fog.

I knew that ominous lull all too well - the Black Dog had come slinking back into our lives.

We'd dealt with his mangy presence before, usually triggered by stressful life events or the mistress's hormones being out of whack. The Black Dog would slink through the doorway unannounced, planting himself stubbornly in the middle of the room as if he belonged there. With each passing day, his menacing shadow would stretch farther into every corner until the entire house felt consumed by his sombre gloom.

Suddenly, simple joys became almost impossible. Getting out of bed was a herculean effort. Enjoyable hobbies and pastimes lay abandoned as apathy took over. I recognised that hollow look in the mistress's eyes—it was the look of someone locked in a dark battle, fighting just to muster the energy to function.

Whenever the Black Dog paid us an unwelcome visit, my job became double-duty. Not only did I provide warm cuddles and furry distraction, but I made sure to stay hyper-vigilant, watching the mistress's every move protectively. I knew from experience that in his cruellest moments, the Black Dog could tempt even the strongest souls with despair so insidious that . . . well, let's just say I wasn't going to let her out of my sight when he was around.

This time, his foul presence seemed to be tied to the kids' move out and our new shrunken pack dynamics. All that unfiltered loneliness and emptiness for the Black Dog to feed upon. The big house that had been the lively hub of our family now felt like hollow emptiness, echoing with phantom memories of happier times. No wonder the mistress seemed adrift in her own sadness.

I did everything a faithful hound could to chase away the unwanted guest—goofy tricks, sloppy kisses, cuddling up tight against her for hourlong Netflix binges. Anything to distract from the Black Dog's toxic whispers. But his grip remained infuriatingly firm, like a demonic houseguest who had overstayed his welcome by several lifetimes.

Then one day, I spotted a spark of the mistress's old spirit. She was doing that "looking intently at laptop" thing again, her eyes brighter than they'd been in months. The Black Dog's spell must have been momentarily broken!

Sure enough, a few days later the big clear-out began. Drawers upturned, closets ransacked, charity shop donations piling up as unused possessions were ruthlessly purged. She was dissatisfied and making a change—the first step to showing the Black Dog the door!

Soon, all the signs were there—the hushed conversations, the house showings. Leave it to Ben and the cats to make this place look lively! Then finally, moving day arrived and we transitioned to a cosy little two bedroom place. Smaller, cleaner, fresher . . . and most importantly, with no room for the Black Dog's draining presence.

The timing turned out to be quite fortunate too, given my own declining health issues. These aging bones were certainly grateful for no more stairs to contend with! Though the hard laminate flooring hasn't been kind to me . . . it seemed like every time I settled in for a snooze, I'd wake up having leaked all over the place. Mortifying for an old dog's dignity, but the mistress always cleaned it up without a fuss. We're in the same creaky, leaky boat together these days.

Mostly though, I'm just glad to see the mistress's smile shining bright again now that the Black Dog has been firmly shown the door. She seems rejuvenated, humming little tunes while she putters about our new compact domain. There's no room for darkness to fester when you've got a cosy, clutter-free burrow to snuggle up in.

Of course, I'll remain ever vigilant should that mangy mutt ever dare to darken our door again. He may think he's achieved a permanent residency in the past, but this old pup will always be here to guard the threshold. Stanch defender of the pack, protector of smiles and sunlight—that's my sacred duty.

So for now, we can all bask in the warm, happy vibes of a fresh start. A new chapter filled with possibilities, securely tucked away in our cheerful little den. And when the Black Dog's shadow looms on the horizon once more, he'll promptly receive a warning bark that this territory is already claimed—by peace, healing, and most of all, love.

The Day I Became a Canine Fashion Icon

Alright, picture this: there I am, minding my own business, enjoying my mid-morning nap in that perfect sunbeam that hits the living room floor. You know the one—it's like the universe's way of saying, "Here's your personal doggy tanning bed, old sport."

Suddenly, the mistress bursts through the front door like she's just won the lottery. Now, usually when she comes home, it's a quick pat on the head and maybe a treat if I play my cards right. But this time? She's practically vibrating with excitement.

"Ben! Look what I've got for you!" she squeals, waving a shopping bag around like it contains the secret to eternal puppyhood.

I haul myself up, joints creaking like an old rocking chair, and give her my best "This better be good, I was having an epic dream about chasing squirrels" look.

She reaches into the bag and pulls out . . . wait for it . . . a hoodie. A dog hoodie. But not just any dog hoodie, oh no. This bad boy has "Adi dog" emblazoned across the back in big, bold letters.

"Isn't it adorable?" she gushes, holding it up for my inspection. "It's like Adidas, but for dogs! Get it?"

Oh, I get it alright. I get that my dignity is about to take a nosedive.

Now, don't get me wrong. I love the mistress more than belly rubs and bacon combined. But sometimes, I swear she forgets I'm a distinguished gentleman of a certain age, not some Instagram-ready puppy influencer.

But hey, who am I to rain on her parade? So I sit there, tail wagging half-heartedly, as she manoeuvres my creaky limbs into this sartorial masterpiece.

"Oh, Ben! You look so handsome!" she coos, stepping back to admire her handiwork.

I catch a glimpse of myself in the hallway mirror and... well, let's just say "handsome" isn't the first word that comes to mind. "Slightly embarrassed old dog trying to relive his glory days" feels more accurate.

But then the master walks in, takes one look at me in my new getup, and bursts out laughing. "Look at you, you old sports star! Ready for your big game, are you?"

And you know what? His laughter is infectious, and I can't help but get caught up in the moment. I start prancing around the living room like I'm walking the red carpet at the Doggy Oscars.

"Work it, Ben!" the mistress cheers as I lounge dramatically on the floor like I'm a furry supermodel, and generally hamming it up for all I'm worth.

And you know what? It's fun. It's ridiculous, sure, but it's fun. For a few minutes, I forget about my creaky joints and greying muzzle. I'm not old Ben, the arthritic family dog. I'm Ben, the canine fashion icon, ready to take on the world one stylish waddle at a time.

The excitement eventually dies down, and life returns to normal. But every now and then, when the mistress is having a rough day, I'll nudge her hand and give her my best "Dress me up, I'm ready for my close-up" look.

Because at the end of the day, isn't that what being part of a family is all about? Sometimes you're the one needing a pick-me-up, and sometimes you're the one wearing a ridiculous outfit to bring a smile to someone's face.

So here's to new adventures, no matter how old you are. Here's to trying new things, even if they make you look a bit silly. And here's to the humans who love us enough to think we look "adorable" in doggy streetwear.

Now, if you'll excuse me, I have a nap to finish. Being a fashion icon is exhausting work, you know.

A Gentle Ramble

My old pal Binx and I have been stretching our legs and getting the lay of the land around our new den. Well, to be perfectly honest, he does most of the stretching while I do a fair bit of puffing and plodding these days.

Don't get me wrong, I absolutely relish the chance to get out and about, putting my nose to the ground to inhale all the intriguing new scents. There's just something about being outdoors that invigorates and delights me, even if I can't quite rip around with the same youthful abandon anymore.

Binx, on the other paw, takes to exploring our fresh territory with utter delight. That kitty was born to ramble! He prances ahead of me on the path, dashing this way and that after tantalising smells and flitting shadows. His tail (perpetually puffed up like a regal plume) swishes back and forth as he navigates the new surroundings with casual confidence.

"C'mon, old bone-bag!" he'll taunt over his shoulder when I lag too far behind. "Are those rickety legs gonna hold up or shall I send for the dog-weight?"

I simply huff in response, too winded to engage in our typical back-and-forth banter. Binx may be getting on in years himself, but he's still spry as a spring kitten compared to my creaky shuffle. I'm increasingly envious of how easily he can scamper up trees and scale fences when the fancy strikes. Movements that used to be second nature for me are now undertaken with great trepidation.

Like going down inclines, for instance. What used to be a simple lope is now a stomach-clenching ordeal where my back legs seem to simply buckle and flail beneath me. More than once I've found myself doing an ungraceful rump-slide down a grassy slope, scrabbling futilely until Binx arrives to lick me clean of dirt and embarrassment.

"Need me to fetch the Rollator for you next time, gramps?" he'll snicker, dodging my attempts to cuff him with a paw. "Maybe put a wee helmet on that noggin too, save what's left of your brains!"

Cheeky git. But I secretly appreciate having him around to supervise my frail constitutionals, even if he'll never admit it out loud. One too many tumbles and I may not be able to get back up on my own.

Still, I refuse to let the indignities of old age stop me from enjoying these outings to the fullest. I may be stooped and wheezy, but by golly I'm going to sniff every flower box and piddle on every tree trunk while I still can! And Binx makes for excellent company, keeping me going with his playful teasing and occasional helpful nudge when I look at risk of keeling over.

We've already scouted out all the prime sun puddle spots for napping, the cosy tucked-away nooks perfect for escaping human nuisances, and let me tell you, the new territory has no shortage of birds to fascinate us! Binx and I will spend hours watching their fluttery antics, him tensed to pounce while my dreams are filled with wistful visions of bounding through fields in pursuit. Not that these old bones could possibly catch them anymore, but one can dream!

On our rambles, I willingly let Binx take the lead while I amble behind at my own creaky pace. He'll pause every so often to ensure I'm still plodding gamely in his wake, ribboning that fluffy tail until I've caught up. I can see the mischievous glee sparkling in his eyes—secretly delighted to be the sturdy one keeping his decrepit pal on track for once.

By the time we circle back home, my tongue is fully lolled out and my paws can barely keep trudging along. But there's a certain hard-won contentment that comes with being happily tuckered out after an adventure, however modest. As I heave myself up onto the porch, I shoot Binx a look of weary gratitude.

Tomorrow I'll be stiff and creaky, no doubt about it. But lounging in a sunbeam with my oldest friend by my side, swapping tales of the big wide world we've seen? Well, there's just nothing better than that.

A Difficult Road Ahead

I'll never forget the look of heartbroken concern on the mistress's face when she found me that morning. I had awoken feeling . . . off. Uncomfortable rumblings and painful cramping in my tummy made it clear something wasn't right.

Before I could even open my mouth to whine for help, the unmistakable feeling of warm liquid between my legs told me it was too late. I had made quite a mess of myself and the bedding around me. How utterly mortifying.

As the mistress cleaned me up, she kept murmuring soothing reassurances that it was okay, that accidents happen, especially with an old pup like me. But the strained tone in her voice revealed her inner worries. We had been noticing my back legs weakening and displaying lack of coordination recently—could this loss of bladder and bowel control be related?

The master wore the same pained expression when he came home and saw the state of me, gently lifting me into the car to pay an urgent visit to the vet clinic. I knew they were both fearing the worst: that my body was beginning to fail me in earnest. As I watched the familiar neighbourhood sights passing by through the window, I silently braced myself to receive whatever difficult news awaited.

Sure enough, after an examination and taking my history into account, the vet diagnosed me with a condition called degenerative myelopathy. A progressive disease that attacks the spinal cord, slowly dimming the pathways that control the legs, bathroom functions, you name it. There is no cure, only managing the symptoms as best we can for as long as possible.

"I'm so sorry," the kind vet said, resting a hand on the mistress's shoulder as she dissolved into tears. "Ben is showing advanced signs of this disease. We can start him on steroids to provide some relief, but . . ." His voice trailed off delicately.

But we all knew what he meant. This would be an inevitably difficult road travelled towards the end. One day, perhaps sooner than any of us wanted, I would lose my mobility and dignity entirely. Would that warrant letting me go to save me from undue suffering?

Not if the mistress had any say in it. Through her tears, she immediately began peppering the vet with questions about accommodations, special diets, waterproof bedding—anything to ensure I could live out my days with comfort and grace.

"He's still got that bright spirit," she insisted, cupping my greying face in her hands. "As long as Ben still wants to keep fighting, we'll be right there with him every step of the way."

I must admit, as the vet loaded me up with medications and lugged me back out to the car, I felt . . . scared. Not for the growing physical discomforts and indignities awaiting me, but for the emotional turmoil and difficult choices this would force on my beloved family. The last thing I'd ever want is to be a burden to them.

But the mistress seems determined that I not give up, that we attack this disease with everything we've got for as long as

I have good quality of life left. As we drove home, her palm stroking my fur, she began rambling about all the adaptations we'd make—puppy pads everywhere, ramps over stairs, orthopaedic beds, scheduling my day around a new routine of medications and activities to keep me engaged.

"We've got this, Benny Boo," she murmured, using that special nickname again. "You've taken such good care of us for all these years. Now it's our turn to take care of you, for as long as we have left together."

I felt immensely grateful for her fierce determination to make me comfortable, no matter how unpleasant and messy things got. At the same time, a tiny kernel of guilt took root deep inside me, worrying about the toll this would take on her. I know how selflessly she gives of herself, how she would run herself ragged ensuring my every need is met.

For now, armed with the steroids and stomach soothers, I do feel a little like my old self again. But I know this disease will only continue its cruel progression, stripping away more of my mobility and bodily functions until I am fully dependent on my family. I cannot fathom how difficult that must be for them.

All I can do is savour each day for the simple joys it brings—a sun-drenched patch to nap in, a favourite toy to gum contentedly, or the feeling of the mistress's arms hugging me close. I'll wag my tail joyfully for as long as I can, seeking out every opportunity to make her smile and laugh likc she used to.

Perhaps that is the greatest gift an old pup like me can give in return: Showing her that even as everything unravels, my spirit remains intact and at peace. Forcing her to remain in good cheer and soak up the sweetness of each moment with her faithful shadow by her side.

It's a heartbreakingly bittersweet journey we've begun, to be sure. But she's determined that my golden years be filled with more warm sun than dark clouds. And with her boundless love lighting the way ahead, I've no doubt she'll make it so.

Leaning on My Pack

These days, getting vertical is quite the ordeal. What used to be as simple as unfolding my legs and pushing up now requires a full-scale production worthy of the theatre!

When I feel the urge to take a stroll or find a new patch of sunbeam to bask in, I'll let out a feeble woof to summon my rescue crew. The master and mistress have become experts at hoisting these old bones, draping a soft towel beneath me to gently leverage me into a standing position.

"Easy does it now, up we go," the mistress will coo, straining against my dead weight while the master gets a firm grip on the other end of the towel.

Together they'll hoist and pull until finally—success! I'm upright, though shakier than a newborn fawn. My back legs intermittently forget how to operate properly, leaving me weaving and stumbling like I've had one too many biscuits from the brew dog. Thank dog for my people being there to steady me, or else I'd crumple right back down in an ungraceful heap.

The mistress has fashioned a sort of makeshift harness out of an old robe belt looped around my middle. She'll clip it on then take the lead, guiding me out the doggy door at a snail's pace so I can patrol the front garden on unsteady stilts. If I'm feeling particularly frisky, we'll make it all the way down the front path to the gate before my legs decide they're done for the day.

"That's quite enough adventure for now, I'd say!" the mistress will laugh, turning us around and through the ritual of lifting and coaxing me back inside.

Gone are the days of freewheeling neighbourhood rambles with my old pal Binx, chasing squirrels and studying every new scent. These days, a toddle out to the shrubs to take care of business is about the extent of my exploring. But I'm just grateful to still be getting fresh air on my face at all!

The mistress has taken every precaution to make our humble den as comfortable and accessible as possible for me. She's invested in an ultra-plush orthopaedic dog bed that hugs my frail bones in sumptuous comfort—no more hard floors leaving me stiff and sore! Layers of cozy blankets keep me toasty, even during my heaviest snoozes when I'm a bit too sleepy to rearrange myself.

And oh, have I mentioned the incontinent britches she's got me kitted out with? Surprisingly not as mortifying as you'd think, and they spare the mistress countless hours of scrubbing accident messes. Just slide the befouled one off, roll me over to my other side, and shimmy a fresh garment on. No fuss, no muss! Well . . . relatively speaking.

"You're being such a good boy, sticking this out with me," she'll whisper fiercely. I know she battles feelings of sadness seeing me so limited these days. But I'll purposely let out a rumbling snore or kick a leg to show her my spirit is very much intact and content.

Because despite my body failing me more each day, I truly don't mind this simpler existence of afternoon naps and mastering the art of being coddled. If I've got my pack surrounding and caring for me every step of the way, doting on me with warmth and love, I want for nothing.

I'm pretty sure that's the secret to remaining a smiling, tail-wagging pupper even as my physical self may unravel—keeping my heart filled to bursting with the reassuring presence of my family. And maybe leaving them just a token souvenir fur tuft here and there, so they never forget I was here.

The Long Goodbye

I'll never forget the pained, heartbroken look on the mistress's face as she cradled me in the back of the car. My poor rear end had once again betrayed me in the most undignified way possible, and we were urgently headed to the vet clinic.

This bout of the diarrhoeas, as the master delicately put it, had hit me like a freight train. No amount of padding up or quick reflexes could contain the explosive results. By the time my abdomen stopped violently cramping, I was left horribly soiled and exhausted.

"It's okay, Benny," the mistress kept whispering, rocking me gently despite the mess. "We're getting you straight to the doctor, you'll feel better soon."

But the grim look in her eyes said it all. We both knew deep down that this was just the latest, foulest manifestation of my degenerating body's slow decline. The medications and accommodations could only do so much for so long.

At the clinic, the caring vet examined me thoroughly as the mistress struggled not to crumple into fresh tears. They murmured in hushed tones, words like "quality of life" and "letting go" and "the kindest option." I knew what that sombre conversation signalled.

GENTLE BEN

For weeks now, we'd all been fighting tooth and nail to keep my aging, ailing self as comfortable and engaged as possible. But now the vet was recommending that they consider the alternative—skipping me gently across the Rainbow Bridge before I suffered any further indignities and pain.

As if in staunch denial, the mistress immediately began peppering the vet with suggestions. What if we changed my diet again? What other medications were there to try? Couldn't we schedule regular fluid therapy sessions to flush out my poor failing body? She rattled off idea after idea, each one more heartbreakingly futile than the last.

With infinite patience and compassion, the vet rested his hand over hers and shook his head. "I truly think Ben has reached the end of what modern medicine can do for him. We've bought him some wonderful extra time, but now the kindest thing may be . . ."

He didn't need to finish that sentence. We all knew what it meant even if we didn't want to say it out loud. The mistress dissolved into fresh sobs, burying her face into my ruff as I licked her cheeks with a soft woof of acceptance.

I could see it in her eyes—part of her had been anticipating, even secretly hoping for, this newly imparted wisdom. As much as she wanted to fight until the bitter end, some deep part of her knew the battle couldn't rage forever. At some point, mere existence wouldn't outweigh the inevitable suffering still awaiting me.

Not wanting to drag out the process, the appointment was made for first thing the next morning. Just one final night together as a pack before I journeyed on to the next adventure.

We returned home in a heavy silence, which swiftly dissolved into a whirlwind of tearful faces arriving to pay their respects. Bronwyn, Jay, Nana Lynda, even my feline pack came in to sniff me over and say their goodbyes.

I soaked in every minute of it, drinking deeply from the warm well of affection and happy memories that sustained our pack. The mistress doted on me relentlessly, letting me gorge on all the naughty treats my old tummy could handle because hey, consequences be damned. Slivers of chicken, nubs of cheese, an entire gravy-smothered biscuit at one point!

We laughed over stories of my mischievous younger days.

As the light faded into evening, the master solemnly scooped me up and carried me up to their bedroom for one final snuggled sleepover. Too frail now to make that climb on my own, but he was determined I spent these precious last hours surrounded by tranquil familiarity.

I drifted in and out of sleep to the reassuring sounds of their quiet snores and the clock's steady ticking rhythm—small familiarities I'd know by heart through the decades. They kept vigil over me until morning's pale light began creeping through the curtains.

While the rest of the house slumbered on, we shared one last hushed communion together, a reverent nuzzling of cheeks and whispered, "I love you." The mistress clutched me fiercely, her tears quickly drenching my ruff, but I met her gaze with perfect understanding. I knew my time had come.

As we headed to the vet's office for the final time, I drank in the sights and smells of my beloved neighbourhood.

This world of ours, so achingly vibrant and beautiful . . . and yet I felt curiously at peace about departing it. My great life's journey had reached its final mile, but what an adventure it had been!

My tail thumped a gentle farewell as I absorbed my family's I love you one last time. Then, surrounded by their warmth and tenderness, I prepared to take my next leap into the great unknown.

Don't be too sad, I wanted to tell them through licks and nuzzles. We'll always be pack, even if I'm watching over you all from afar after today. Just as you've showered me with love unconditional, that sacred bond remains forever...

Thank you for the grandest life a good boy like me could ever hope for. Until we're reunited once more, keep smiling and wagging—for me.

Life's Greatest Comforts

Take heart, my sweet family, for while our parting leaves an empty space in your den, cherished memories will forever fill it with warmth and light.

Yes, the silent absence of my cheerful tail-thumps may echo cavernously at first. But quickly you'll find those halls replenished by recollections—slobbery wake up calls, living room zoomies, my clumsy destruction of all things chewable! Endearing images to make you chuckle through fresh pangs of missing me.

When you find yourselves instinctively moving to give me a good ear scratch, only to be met with vacant air, think back to all the goofy pre-treats dances and tricks I'd perform solely for your amusement. Pure canine comedy gold, meant to coax your spirits into joyful buoyancy in even the dreariest moments.

And on those melancholy nights when the stillness feels too vast, when you mistake a random creak for my impending click-clack of nails across the floorboards, let warm memories of our snuggled slumbers come rushing in. How I'd faithfully make the nightly rounds of kid's bedrooms, keeping watchful four-legged vigils to chase away terrors until sunny dawns crested.

Such was ever my noble role, that of faithful life-companion and protector of my pack's peace of mind. For what deeper contentment could a good pup hope to bring than the incomparable comforts of soul-deep loyalty, security, nonjudgmental affection? To be at once your dearest friend, shoulder to cry on, source of unbridled mirth in dark times?

Yes, perhaps when all is said and done, being a dog is the most sacred of all life's paths. For we represent life's purest joys—living zestfully in each new moment, finding boundless delight in even the simplest pleasures. Chasing sunbeams, greeting every dawn with tail-wagging enthusiasm, savouring all the smells and tastes and tactile wonders this earth has to offer.

We have no room for grudges or angst or existential dread. Only an abiding sense of gratitude for the chance to love you all unconditionally in this shared experience called life. To protect you when needed, to shower you with steadfast companionship and mirth. No airs, no facade, just guileless authenticity—that is a good pup's credo.

So while my soul may have outgrown its earthly form, you must believe that it goes on, still chasing sunbeams on brilliant fields amid the Rainbows Bridge's eternal spring. I've merely reunited with the great cosmic dog park in the sky, romping alongside all my predecessors in unburdened revelry. Awaiting with wags a-twitching for that joyful day when you'll rejoin me, your footfalls and laughter making my spiritual ears prick up in sublime anticipation!

In the meantime, know that even though our physical frolicking's have ceased for now, you'll never truly lack for my essence while your heart remains filled with our special recollections. I'm still there in spirit whenever:

* You smile over a particularly fond snapshot—my furry grinning mug peering out, radiating glee.

* You catch a fuzzy wayward tuft of my fur clinging to the furniture, prompting you to scoop it up and bring it close for an appreciative snuggle.

* You run your fingers along the plaster impression of my paw print memorial and feel that familiar size, shape, and heft that used to pamper your lap so regularly.

* You hold the frame containing my earthly remains, physical vessels now empty yet brimming with cherished memory husks of a life beautifully lived and loved.

These lasting talismans are powerful evocations of all we shared and the lasting impact even a simple house pup can indelibly etch across soulful owners' hearts. So hold them dear, let them be perpetual reminders that just as I brought you all incomparable light, your own radiant spirits shall be my eternal guides along the planes we now walk asunder.

Remember me with smiles for the joy-serving doofus I was, not with corrosive tears over what is lost. Our bond remains transcendent, ineffable, never amended. And while this mortal parting was the hardest decision to make, it was ultimate testament to the benevolence of your selfless devotion.

"The risk of love is loss" was the mortal maxim that kept many from giving themselves over to a canine soulmate like myself these many moons. Yet you opened your hearts unreservedly, showering this pup with care, sustenance, and affection to enrich us both beyond quantification.

So no, my friends, this is no ending but merely Intermission—a chance to revel in all we co-created before the next chapter in eternity's epic for us all takes deliriously joyful shape. Get ready for slobbery reunions, zestful waggering, and cosmic abound! I'll warm up my finest vocals for orisons of unbridled celebration.

For now though, savour those simple human joys that so delighted me—the crisp turn of new book pages, savoured snacks fresh from the oven, sunbeams to lounge in languidly. Live vividly, insouciantly, as I did. For in honouring my blithesome spirit, you honour the greatest gift that dog and humankind can bestow: Perfect love, in this imperfect present.

Until we romp anew, my wonderful pack, stay ever wagging . . .

A Heart's Farewell

The silence in the house is deafening. It's been days since we said goodbye to Ben, but the void he left behind seems to grow larger with each passing moment. I find myself wandering from room to room, expecting to hear the familiar click of his nails on the hardwood floor or the soft thump of his tail against the wall. But there's only silence now, punctuated by my own muffled sobs.

The decision to let Ben go was the hardest I've ever had to make. Even now, the memory of that final moment in the vet's office haunts me. The second his heart stopped beating, a tidal wave of regret crashed over me. I wanted to scream, to beg the universe for a do-over, to turn back time and bring my beloved boy back. But it was too late. The finality of it all was crushing.

For days, I've been battling with guilt, questioning every aspect of my decision. Was it too soon? Could we have tried one more treatment? Did I give up on him? The 'what ifs' are relentless, gnawing at my conscience and keeping me awake at night. I've cried more tears than I thought possible, my eyes swollen and raw from the constant onslaught of grief.

But as the initial shock begins to subside, I'm slowly allowing myself to remember Ben as he was before the illness took hold. I think about the quality of life he had in his final days—the struggle to stand, the loss of dignity, the pain that clouded his once-bright eyes. And I know, in my heart of hearts, that letting him go was the right thing to do. It wasn't just the right choice—it was the only choice a loving owner could make.

Painful as it was, it was an act of love. The final, most selfless gift I could give to the creature who had given me nothing but unconditional love and joy for so many years.

As I leaf through old photo albums, I'm struck by how blessed my life has been because of Ben. From the day we brought him home as a bouncing, three year old to his twilight years as a dignified, grey-muzzled elder statesman, he filled our lives with laughter, love, and unwavering loyalty. He was there for every milestone, every triumph, every heartbreak. He was more than just a pet—he was family.

I know that no dog can ever replace what Ben was to us. The thought of welcoming another furry friend into our home feels impossible right now. The wound is too fresh, the loss too raw. Maybe someday, when the pain has dulled to a manageable ache, we'll be ready to open our hearts again. But for now, I'm content to honour Ben's memory and work through my grief at my own pace.

In the meantime, I find solace in the feline members of our household. Ember, Simba and Nala, who knew and loved Ben in their own cat-like way, seem to sense the shift in the household's energy. They've been extra affectionate lately, as if trying to fill the gap left behind by their canine companion.

And then there's Binx—dear, roguish Binx. Ben's unlikely best friend, the cat who thought he was a dog. I see the loss in Binx's eyes too, a quiet mourning for his fallen comrade. Yet, true to his nature, Binx soldiers on. He still goes for his daily walks patrolling the neighbourhood as if he and Ben were still a team keeping watch over their territory.

Watching Binx navigate this new reality reminds me that life goes on, even in the face of profound loss. It's a bittersweet comfort, but a comfort nonetheless.

As I close the photo album and wipe away a fresh wave of tears, I find myself drawn to the small memorial we've created for Ben in the corner of our living room. There, in a beautiful wooden frame, sits a collection of his most precious mementos. His paw prints, a small lock of his soft fur, carefully clipped and preserved. And at the centre, a photo frame containing his ashes, surrounded by pictures of Ben at his happiest—chasing balls in the park, lounging in his favourite sunny spot, and cuddled up close to us.

As I gaze at this tribute to our beloved friend, I'm reminded of the Rainbow Bridge. It's a concept that's brought me comfort in these dark days—the idea of a paradise where pets wait for their human companions after they've passed on. I imagine Ben there now, young and healthy again, running and playing with all the other beloved animals who've gone before him. Waiting patiently, as he always did, for the day when we'll be reunited.

I find myself whispering a quiet thank you to the universe for bringing Ben into our lives. For thirteen wonderful years, he was the heart of our home, the glue that held us together through good times and bad. His physical presence may be gone, but the love he left behind will never fade.

Goodbye, my sweet boy. Thank you for the joy, the laughter, the unconditional love. Thank you for the muddy paw prints on the kitchen floor and the cuddles. Thank you for being you, in all your perfect imperfection.

You were the best of dogs, the most loyal of friends, the gentlest of souls. And though the pain of losing you is almost unbearable, I wouldn't trade a single moment of our time together.

Rest easy, Ben. Until we meet again at the Rainbow Bridge, know that you are loved, you are missed, and you will never be forgotten.

In the softening light of the evening, I feel a gentle breeze ruffle my hair. For just a moment, I could swear I hear the faint jingle of a collar, the soft pant of a happy dog. And I smile through my tears, knowing that in some way, somehow, Ben is still with us. Not in body, perhaps, but in every memory, every laugh, every moment of love we shared.

And in that, I find peace.

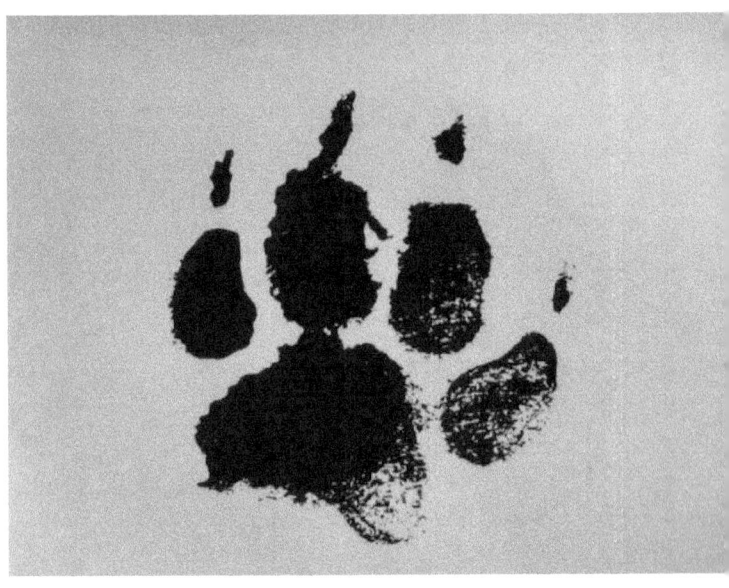

Epilogue

The decision to euthanise a pet is never taken lightly. According to the British Veterinary Association (BVA), there are several factors that pet owners and veterinary surgeons consider when making this difficult choice [1]:

1. Is the pet's condition chronic, terminal, or causing unmanageable pain?

2. Has the pet's quality of life deteriorated significantly?

3. Are there any reasonable treatment options left that could improve the pet's condition?

4. Can the family provide the necessary care and financial resources for ongoing treatment?

In Ben's case, the answer to these questions had become painfully clear. His hind legs shuddered and collapsed beneath him without warning, as if the nerves simply forgot to remind the muscles to engage. He felt nothing from the pelvis down, only a strange sort of numbness. The signal-callers in his spine had gone dark and haywire.

Indignities continued to pile up as his bladder and bowels betrayed him without notice or control. He was left to awkwardly lie in potent puddles of his own making, a once proud dog diminished to cowering embarrassment. Tail episodically thumping in shame, apologising to us with remorseful eyes.

Euthanasia is a way to end an animal's suffering when there's no hope for recovery or a good quality of life. It's not giving up on a pet, but rather a final act of love to prevent unnecessary pain and distress.

The impact of this decision ripples through the entire family, affecting everyone in different ways.

Emotionally, the decision to euthanise a pet can bring forth a tidal wave of feelings: grief, guilt, relief, and sometimes even anger. The Blue Cross, a UK animal charity, emphasises that these emotions are all normal parts of the grieving process [2]. We often struggle with feelings of guilt, questioning if we made the right choice or if we could have done more. It's important for us to remember that choosing euthanasia out of love and compassion is not a betrayal, but a final act of kindness.

Physically, the stress and grief associated with losing a pet can manifest in various ways. Symptoms like loss of appetite, difficulty sleeping, and a general feeling of fatigue. The PDSA (People's Dispensary for Sick Animals) notes that these physical responses to grief are common and typically subside as the healing process progresses [3].

For children, the loss of a pet through euthanasia can be particularly challenging. It's often their first experience with death, and they may struggle to understand why their furry friend can't be "fixed" like a broken toy. The RSPCA (Royal Society for the Prevention of Cruelty to Animals) recommends several strategies to help children cope with pet loss [4]:

1. Be honest and use clear, age-appropriate language to explain the situation.

2. Allow children to be involved in the decision-making process when appropriate.

3. Encourage them to express their feelings and memories about their pet.

4. Consider creating a memorial or ritual to honour the pet's life.

5. Reassure children that it's okay to feel sad and that the pain will lessen over time.

As for pets like Ben, they may not fully grasp the concept of euthanasia, but they do sense the emotional turmoil it causes to their human family. They often pick up on their stress and sadness, which can lead to changes in their own behaviour or mood. The best thing humans can do for their remaining pets during this time is to maintain as much normalcy as possible in their routines while also offering extra comfort and reassurance.

It's a heavy topic, to be sure, but one that I believe is important for all pet owners to consider and discuss openly. By understanding the factors involved in making this decision and preparing for its emotional impact, families can approach this difficult situation with compassion, clarity, and the knowledge that they're acting out of love for their furry companions.

As we approached the final moments, I'm reminded to share with you the importance of being present during a pet's euthanasia, even though it is the most difficult and painful of experiences for the family left behind. As stressed by the Blue Cross [5]. There are several reasons for this:

1. Comfort and reassurance: Your presence can help keep your pet calm and comfortable in their final moments.

2. Closure: Being there allows you to say a proper goodbye and can aid in the grieving process.

3. Ensuring peace: You can witness firsthand that your pet's passing is peaceful and pain-free.

4. Preventing distress: Some pets may become anxious if left alone in an unfamiliar environment.

To help cope with the difficult decision and the grief that follows, here are some tips from various UK animal welfare organisations:

1. Seek support: Don't hesitate to lean on friends, family, or professional counsellors. The Blue Cross offers a Pet Bereavement Support Service [6].

2. Create a memorial: This could be a photo album, a special garden spot, or a donation to an animal charity in your pet's name [7].

3. Take care of yourself: Grief can be physically exhausting. Remember to eat well, get enough sleep, and exercise [8].

4. Allow yourself to grieve: There's no 'right' way to mourn. Give yourself permission to feel sad, angry, or even relieved [9].

In the end, what matters most is the love and care we receive throughout our lives. And while the thought of saying goodbye is never easy, I know that Ben took comfort in knowing that his family would make such a difficult decision only out of the deepest love and concern for his well-being, and that they were there with him until the very end.

References:

[1] British Veterinary Association. (2019). "When it's time to say goodbye - Advice for pet owners on euthanasia." https://www.bva.co.uk/take-action/our-campaigns/euthanasia/

[2] Blue Cross. (2021). "Coping with the loss of a pet." https://www.bluecross.org.uk/pet-advice/coping-loss-pet

[3] PDSA. (2021). "Coping with pet bereavement." https://www.pdsa.org.uk/taking-care-of-your-pet/looking-after-your-pet/all-pets/coping-with-pet-bereavement

[4] RSPCA. (2020). "Helping children cope with the loss of a pet." https://www.rspca.org.uk/adviceandwelfare/pets/bereavement/children

[5] Blue Cross. (2021). "Pet euthanasia: Staying with your pet at the end."

[6] Blue Cross. (2021). "Pet Bereavement Support Service."

[7] PDSA. (2021). "Memorialising your pet."

[8] Cats Protection. (2020). "Coping with the loss of a cat."

[9] Dogs Trust. (2021). "Coping with losing a dog."

Don't miss out!

Visit the website below and you can sign up to receive emails whenever Kirsty F. McKay publishes a new book. There's no charge and no obligation.

https://books2read.com/r/B-A-IWAZ-FRSRD

BOOKS 2 READ

Connecting independent readers to independent writers.

Also by Kirsty F. McKay

The Morvantia Chronicles
The Veils of Valoria
Guardians of Valoria

Standalone
Gentle Ben

About the Author

Kirsty McKay, born in Middlesbrough in 1976, is an author driven by a lifelong passion for writing. From a young age, she immersed herself in the world of books, frequenting the library every week and devouring stories from various genres. While she appreciates all types of literature, Kirsty's heart lies in the realms of fantasy and the paranormal, where her imagination soars.

With a loving marriage spanning twenty seven years, Kirsty is the proud parent of three children and dotes on her four grandchildren.

Kirsty's writing journey took flight when she joined a writing development group, igniting her creative spark. After the publication of her first book, The Veils Of Valoria, The Chronicles of Morvantia Series, she founded The Book Dragon, a platform dedicated to self-published and independently published authors. Fuelled by her frustration of the lack of support for self-published and indie authors,

Kirsty is passionate about nurturing fellow writers and helping them achieve their dreams, while keeping hope aflame. Since its inception on 4 July 2022, The Book Dragon has grown into an award-winning business, fostering a supportive community, and providing abundant opportunities.

Despite managing Fibromyalgia and Osteoarthritis, Kirsty seamlessly weaves her disability into her work, thanks to the unwavering support of her family.

Kirsty is a Reiki Practitioner and a Crystal therapist. Grounded in her Pagan philosophy, Kirsty embraces values and practices that resonate with her core beliefs, drawing upon her clairvoyant abilities in her healing work.

In her spiritual journey, Kirsty finds guidance from her Spirit Guide, Charles, who she lovingly describes as a young Mel Gibson lookalike, and who was an American Quaker in the 1600's that she was married to in a previous life. She also connect with Jack, a loveable scoundrel, and a renowned Galleon Sea Captain in his time, who playfully teases Kirsty about her distinct lack of sea legs.

Kirsty's life is a tapestry woven with creativity, compassion, and unwavering dedication to empowering others through her words and actions.

About the Publisher

Welcome to The Book Dragon Ltd, a publishing company committed to championing the voices of self-published and indie authors. We understand the unique challenges faced by these talented individuals and are dedicated to providing a platform for their work to shine. With our passion for storytelling and unwavering support for independent voices, we strive to foster a community that celebrates creativity and empowers authors to share their stories with the world. Join us on this exciting journey as we bring exceptional literary works from self-published and indie authors to readers worldwide.

Address: Book Dragon Ltd, 6 West Row, Stockton on Tees, TS18 1BT, United Kingdom

Facebook: www.facebook.com/thebookdragonteam

Open to Submissions – Fiction All Genres, Adults & Children's Books, Non -Fiction & Poetry

Supporting Self Published and Independently Published Authors

Editor in Chief: Tim Marshall

Email: tim@thebookdragon.co.uk

Business Executive & Founder: Kirsty F. McKay

Email: kirsty@thebookdragon.co.uk

Testimonials:

The Book Dragon's commitment to supporting Indie and Self-published authors is unmatched, and their selection of books is sure to have something for everyone. I highly recommend this bookstore to anyone looking for their next great read or to any author looking for business support. **Author Eleanor Dixon**

I really appreciate The Book Dragon's support of indie authors and all the creative ways they employ to drive that support. **Author Wayne Kramer**

The Book Dragon is an amazing partner and I am so grateful to be working with such a dedicated and passionate team, devoted to self-published and indie authors. Thank you for everything you do and keep up the good work. **Author Fiona Lowry**

Read more at https://www.thebookdragon.co.uk/.

www.ingramcontent.com/pod-product-compliance
Lightning Source LLC
LaVergne TN
LVHW051039080426
835508LV00019B/1608